Beyond Wealth : How to Get so Rich You Question The Meaning of Making Money

Leon Reeves

Published by Leon Reeves, 2025.

BEYOND WEALTH : HOW TO GET SO RICH YOU QUESTION THE MEANING OF MAKING MONEY

First edition. July 6, 2025.

ISBN: 979-8231425747

Written by Leon Reeves.

Table of Contents

Introduction

You know that feeling when you wake up and the first thing on your mind is money? It's a relentless grind, right? You strive for the next chance, the next promotion, or the next contract. The worst part is this: what if I told you that becoming wealthy isn't the ultimate goal? This is only the start. What your money truly represents in your life is more important than how much you earn.

Let's be honest. We've been taught that having money makes you happy. You put forth a lot of effort, save money, invest, and believe that one day you will succeed. Everyone in this race is displaying their glistening prizes and declaring themselves the victors, including you. But you can sense the emptiness seeping in from the bottom of your heart. What if I told you that your perspective on money is equally as important as your possessions?

People battling their way up the social scale at the expense of their relationships, health, and even sanity is something I have witnessed innumerable times. They believe they're done once they reach the six-figure barrier. They aren't, spoiler warning. My buddy, it's a slippery slope. After you reach one milestone, another one is just around the corner. Like a mirage in the desert, it appears farther away the closer you go, even when you believe you're getting close.

However, the fact is that wealth is the means, not the end goal. What counts is what you do with it. You may purchase freedom, alternatives, and even a small amount of comfort with money. However, you will eventually run into a wall. You'll be surrounded by all of this things, including houses, automobiles, and maybe even a yacht, and you'll be left wondering why everything seems so empty. You may wonder, "Is this it?"

You see, when you begin to wonder what money actually means, the game changes. You start to see the wider picture rather than chasing after the next dollar. You come to understand that the most rewarding things in life—experiences, connections, and personal development—cannot be bought with a credit card. Indeed, they need investment, but the money is in the form of time, effort, and emotional vitality.

Imagine for a moment that your value isn't just determined by your money account. Imagine waking up each day with the knowledge that your influence on the world is considerably greater than your wealth. Everything changes when your goal is to create value rather than amass cash. You begin creating something that embodies your ideals and your self, something that endures.

The goal of this book is to dispel the myths around riches and money. It's about focusing on the important things. I will teach you how to think differently about money, how to generate and grow your income, and how to change the way you feel about wealth in general. Warning: there will be messiness. You'll need to face your convictions, anxieties, and even shortcomings. But let's be honest: you can't avoid the difficult things if you plan to stick with this for the long run.

We will explore the psychology of abundance in great detail. It's not enough to be optimistic and wish for the best. It's about radically changing your perspective on the world. Developing an abundant attitude makes it easier to recognize possibilities everywhere. You begin to see life as a partnership rather than a competition. You realize that everyone has plenty and that your achievement doesn't take away from anybody else's.

Another crucial topic we'll discuss is adding value to the marketplace. Solving actual problems is more important than simply selling products. Money is a result of your efforts when you concentrate on producing true worth. The fact that you're giving them something they actually need makes them eager to pay. The magic takes place there.

The best way to maximize your efforts is to scale your revenue sources. One source of income is no longer sufficient. You must innovate, automate, and diversify. Making money isn't the only goal here; you also want to put up processes that work for you, not the other way around. You must have an entrepreneurial mindset, constantly searching for the next chance to make money.

Let's now discuss creating a robust company. You must have a strong foundation, which entails being an expert in marketing and sales. These are essential to every endeavor. You won't make it if you can't sell. However, selling isn't a bad term. The goal is to establish a connection with others and provide them with something of value. When you change your perspective on sales, you'll discover that the transformation is more important than the transaction.

Mastery of finances is yet another crucial component. Making money is only one aspect of it; another is efficiently managing it. You must comprehend the fundamentals of financial literacy, including investing and budgeting. As you increase your fortune, you must safeguard it. It's similar to erecting a castle around your kingdom because, believe me, there are many hazards and diversions in the world.

The worst part, though, is that as you get richer, you have to start considering your goals outside of making money. With all that money, what are you actually doing? What effects are you having on the world? Being philanthropic is an attitude, not merely something for the wealthy. When you start giving back, you'll see that changing the world, not simply expanding your bank account, is what truly fulfills you.

You will reinterpret what success means to you on this trip. The legacy you leave behind is more important than the awards or medals. You will begin to view your riches as a positive instrument. The funds aren't just for you; they're also for the people you love, the causes you care about, and the experiences you wish to share.

This book isn't your typical book on earning money. This manifesto asks you to consider the true meaning of riches in order to live a richer life. I'm not here to try to pitch you on some secret recipe. I'm here to push you beyond your comfort zone, to challenge you, and to get you thinking. Together, let's take this adventure if you're willing to get uncomfortable and dig deep.

You will be getting your hands filthy. You will not succeed. But you know what? It's a step in the process. Accept it. Take anything away from it. Take it and turn it into stepping stones to something bigger. You'll find that the true riches are found in the journey itself as you sort through the complexity of money and purpose.

So, fasten your seatbelt. I can assure you that it will be worth the crazy adventure you are about to go on. Prepare to change your perspective, provide value, increase your revenue, become financially savvy, and discover your calling. This is about living a life that challenges your preconceived notions about everything; it's not just about money.

Chapter 1
The Psychology of Abundance

Shifting Your Mindset

Most likely, you're sitting there thinking what having an abundant mindset actually entails. The harsh reality is that the majority of people are trapped in a state of shortage. They operate under the premise that there isn't enough for everyone. And that attitude? It's a jail. You convince yourself that you need to work harder to achieve your goals while vying for scraps every day when you get up. That's a surefire way to end up burned out, I tell you.

Everything changes when you adopt an abundant attitude. Where others see obstacles, you start to see opportunity. You reach a new level of thinking the instant you understand that everyone can have enough money, success, and happiness and that the world isn't trying to get you. You shift your attention from what you lack to what you can produce.

Having more money is a common misconception about plenty, but it's much more than that. It all comes down to how you live your life. Relationships, experiences, and personal development are all important. You can have a wealth of contacts, expertise, and abilities. To live an affluent life, you don't need a sizable bank account. It's all about acknowledging and valuing the abundance that surrounds you.

The social conditioning is one of the most significant obstacles you will encounter during this transition. We've learned to compare, compete, and keep score. It eats away at you when you browse social media and watch your pals having the time of their life. You ask yourself, "Why don't I have that?" The scarcity mindset is speaking at that point. The reality? Your accomplishment is not diminished by theirs. Your losses are not their victories. Instead of hating people, start enjoying them. You'll be astounded at how much opportunity just one small adjustment may present.

Let us now delve further. You need to clarify your financial principles. Many individuals believe that having money is a sign of greed or that it is bad. Thinking like that keeps you broke—financially and emotionally. Simply said, money is a tool. It enhances your current identity. You can do more good with money if you're a nice person. It will just offer you more opportunities to be a jerk if you already are. Thus, become used to the concept of riches. Accept it. Give yourself permission to desire more guilt-free. The more you develop, the more you can assist others in developing as well.

Your surroundings are an additional component. The five individuals you spend the most time with determine who you are. What happens if you're surrounded by folks who think in terms of scarcity? You will also acquire that thinking. Make an effort to find individuals who believe differently than you do—those who push you to broaden your ideas, excite you, and challenge you. Be in an environment of wealth, surround oneself with achievers, and look for mentors.

Additionally, you must alter the way you speak to yourself. Self-talk has the potential to be both your greatest ally and your worst adversary. You'll stay stuck if you're always criticizing yourself or questioning your skills. Turn the page. Begin by confirming your potential and ability. "I am capable of doing this." "I'm worthy of success." "I can have a lot of things." These aren't simply catchphrases; they're a brand-new brain operating system. Over time, they change the way you think, allowing you to take actions that are consistent with your objectives.

Let's also discuss thankfulness. It may sound cliche, but it's revolutionary. You divert your attention from your shortcomings when you are thankful for what you have. Make appreciation a regular habit. Every day, list three things for which you are grateful. Simple things like a satisfying dinner, a cozy bed, or the fact that you woke up this morning might be considered them. You will begin to notice wealth everywhere as you educate your mind to perceive it in your life.

The next step is to confront your concerns. Fear is a strong feeling that might prevent you from taking advantage of chances. Consider the following: "What could go wrong?" It's usually not as horrible as you imagine. Even if you could fail, it's a necessary part of the process. Accept it. Every setback serves as an experience-based education. You'll feel more in control the more you face your concerns.

Reframe your failures as opportunities for success. The greats—the people you admire—had to overcome hardships to get to where they are today. As a result, they gained knowledge, adjusted, and eventually prospered. Take calculated risks instead of avoiding them. Place modest wagers. Step outside of your comfort zone. You increase your potential for growth each time. You begin to develop resilience, which is essential for an abundant attitude.

Changing your definition of success is another essential change. Success is typically viewed as a straight line: obtain a job, earn money, and retire. However, life is a sequence of curves, dips, and unexpected bends rather than a straight line. Rethink what success means to you. How does it appear? Is it profound connections, fulfilling employment, or financial freedom? You may seek achievement without the burden of social expectations when you establish your own standards. You take charge of creating your own life.

The idea of giving comes next. Giving, whether in the form of time, money, or expertise, creates wealth in your life. The paradox is that you get more when you give more. It's about building relationships and connections, not about charity. You are sowing seeds for your own future when you invest in other people. These relationships may open doors you never would have thought possible.

And let's not overlook education. Growth and curiosity are the foundations of an abundant mindset. Don't be content with what you already know. Make an investment in yourself. Read books, enroll in classes, look for mentors, and go to seminars. Make a commitment to lifelong education. Your ability to add value to the world increases with your level of knowledge. It benefits both parties.

Additionally, you should learn to be patient. It takes time for plenty to develop. It's not a sprint; it's a marathon. Building experiences, connections, and riches takes time. Have faith in the process and practice self-compassion. Your personal development will be derailed the instant you begin comparing your first chapter to someone else's twenty-first. Celebrate the little victories along the way and keep your eyes on the road.

Let's now discuss commitment. It takes commitment to have an abundant attitude. There may be days when you want to give up and feel like everything is too much. Remember why you started on such days. Remember your vision and objectives. Continue moving forward. Your suffering is frequently the first step toward development. Accept it. Allow it to motivate you.

Lastly, surround yourself with abundance-related reminders. Make your surroundings reflect the attitude you wish to adopt. Decorate your area with sayings, pictures, and objects that motivate you. Allow them to act as constant reminders that the world has more than enough. You actively contribute to the creation of your world rather than merely watching it happen.

Every aspect of your life will see a rippling effect once you make the commitment to change your perspective. You'll draw in more possibilities, forge closer bonds with others, and eventually design a life that reflects your ideals. It's about changing the way you think about success and money. You're creating a meaningful and purposeful life instead of merely pursuing financial gain.

It is a decision to adopt an abundant attitude. It's a choice to have faith in possibilities instead of constraints. It's a readiness to confront your anxieties, change your opinions, and make a commitment to personal development. It involves seeing life from a perspective of opportunity rather than scarcity. What is stopping you, then? Venture into the realm of plenty. Accept everything's dirt, confusion, and beauty. We need to rethink what it means to be genuinely wealthy.

1.1 Overcoming Limiting Beliefs

Let's go right to the point: having limited views is what keeps you bound to mediocrity. They are the inner voices that tell you things like, "You'll never be good enough," or "You can't do that." Like a constant background hum, these ideas are so embedded in us that we are unaware of their existence. You must be prepared to listen to those voices and examine what is truly preventing you from moving forward.

"Yeah, I know I have some doubts, but everyone does," you may be thinking. Everyone has doubts, of course, but how you respond to them makes a big difference. You may either face those doubts head-on or allow them to guide your behavior. The majority of individuals choose the easy route, letting their anxieties guide them. "I'd love to start that business, but I'm not sure it'll work," they would remark. That is both a limiting and deadly notion.

Let's be clear: no one is born believing they are incapable of succeeding. It is a learned characteristic rather than an inherited one. As children, we have a lot of dreams. We believe we can be rock stars, astronauts, or whatever else we may dream of. However, life happens. The demands of society drag you down, you hear "no" enough times, and all of a sudden you're confined. You begin to think that such aspirations are unattainable and belong to someone else. It's absurd. That is something you must unlearn.

Determine your limiting beliefs first. Put them in writing. Examine what you're telling yourself in detail. Perhaps you think you lack the necessary abilities to launch a business or that you will never have enough money. Bring it to light, whatever it may be. Recognize it. Recognition is powerful. You may question your views after you've given them a name.

Here's a quick exercise: list the arguments against each limiting belief. If you believe that your lack of a degree prevents you from starting a firm, keep in mind that many successful businesspeople have achieved success without a formal education. Experience, perseverance, and a will to learn are sometimes more valuable than qualifications, according to research. You'll start to notice the holes in your limiting beliefs' basis when you start using facts to refute them.

Let's now discuss reframing. Here's where the magic takes place. Say "How can I afford that?" rather than "I can't afford that." Turn your attention from constraints to opportunities. Your brain gets rewired to think differently as a result of this straightforward linguistic shift. It provides access to an entirely new range of options. By posing the question "how," you're encouraging innovation. You're actively searching for solutions to overcome rather than passively accepting loss.

Visualization is another crucial technique for getting over limiting beliefs. Imagine the life you wish to lead. Shut your eyes and visualize yourself accomplishing your objectives. Experience the feelings that accompany that achievement. The goal of visualization is to teach your mind to accept your dreams as genuine, not simply some woo-woo technique. Regular visualization trains your brain to seek for chances that fit those objectives.

You must be persistent in this exercise. Make time every day to envision who you want to be in the future. Imagine who is around you, what you are doing, and how you are feeling. Construct a clear mental image, then start working to make it a reality.

The importance of self-talk should not be disregarded. It matters how you talk to yourself. You're strengthening those limiting ideas if you're always criticizing yourself or questioning your skills. Start using affirmations to counteract your negative self-talk. Use phrases such as "I am capable." I'm resourceful. I deserve to be successful. At first, it can seem corny, but believe me, it works. Your mind is paying attention.

It's also very important to surround oneself with the appropriate individuals. The five individuals you spend the most time with determine who you are. You will absorb the energy of those who are dreamy but lack ambition if you spend time with them. Seek for those who encourage you to think more broadly and who challenge you. You want pals who will confront your limiting views and prevent you from becoming complacent. Look for mentors who have experienced the road you want to take. Take inspiration from their accomplishments and learn from them.

Additionally, you will need to face your fears. This is about confronting your limiting ideas, not just admitting they exist. Fear is a strong feeling that, if allowed, may paralyze you. What could possibly go wrong, ask yourself? The worst-case situation is usually not quite as awful as you may believe. Of course, you may fail. But what the heck? A stepping stone on the road to success is failure. Accept it. Take anything away from it. Proceed.

This is the point at which action is necessary. You may spend all day discussing how to overcome limiting ideas, but nothing will change if you don't act on it. Begin modestly. Establish attainable objectives and address each one individually. You gain momentum each time you overcome a limiting notion. You reaffirm that you are more capable than you previously believed.

Note all of your victories, no matter how minor. Honor them. These triumphs will remind you of what you are capable of. They will demonstrate that your actions, not your history, define who you are.

Adopting a learner's perspective is another effective tactic. This entails seeing obstacles as chances for development rather than dangers. Refrain from seeing a setback as a failure. Consider it feedback. What can this experience teach you? How can you modify your strategy? This change in viewpoint will assist you in destroying the notion that you are insufficient.

You must also understand the value of perseverance. You will encounter obstacles, but perseverance is essential. It's about picking yourself up after being knocked down by life. Recognize that there is rarely a direct path to achievement. Along the route, there will be obstacles, diversions, and bumps. But you'll persevere if you're determined to get rid of your restricting beliefs.

Continue to remind yourself of your motivation. What makes you desire to be successful? What are your ultimate objectives? It is simpler to overcome uncertainties when you firmly establish your aim. Knowing your why will help you stay motivated and keep your eyes on the goal.

Another option is to use journaling as a self-reflection method. Put your ideas, worries, and limiting beliefs in writing. Put everything on paper. Then, question those assumptions. Consider if they are factual or only stories you have been told. Writing in a journal can help you analyze your ideas and identify the underlying causes of your restricting beliefs.

Immersion in learning is another successful strategy. Attend workshops, enroll in classes, and read books. Increase the scope of your knowledge. Your confidence grows as you gain more knowledge. Limiting beliefs can be effectively countered by knowledge. Self-doubt will be less likely to affect you if you believe you have the appropriate resources and understanding.

Not to be overlooked is the importance of having reasonable expectations. Aiming high is admirable, but avoid setting unrealistic expectations for yourself. Divide your most ambitious objectives into more doable, smaller activities. In this manner, you may gain confidence as you proceed and acknowledge your progress along the way.

Examine the narratives you are telling yourself. Do they empower or de-empower people? Are they helping you achieve your objectives or getting in the way? Rewrite those stories. Tell them tales of success, resiliency, and development.

Everything changes when you view your journey as a series of experiments rather than failures. You start to understand that each failure is really another piece of information on your journey to achievement. You're learning, not failing.

One last piece of advice: accept discomfort. Growth occurs when you step beyond of your comfort zone. You are expanding yourself each time you overcome your limiting beliefs and concerns. You're becoming more capable. Accept the pain; it's an indication that you're headed in the correct way.

When you face your limiting beliefs with purpose and action, they are defeated. What is feasible for you can be redefined by you. Begin now. Determine those beliefs, confront them, and act upon them. You get closer to living a life that fulfills your potential with every step you take to overcome them. Although the journey won't be simple, it will be worthwhile. You are the only one who can set boundaries. Let's liberate you and begin creating the life you deserve.

1.2 Embracing a Growth-Oriented Perspective

Let's get started right away: a growth-oriented viewpoint is the game-changer you were unaware you required. The importance of mentality cannot be emphasized, even though you've heard it before. You need to change your perspective if you want to get so wealthy that you begin to wonder what money is all about. It involves embracing a mindset that thrives on development, education, and the unrelenting quest of progress rather than merely maintaining an optimistic outlook.

Consider it this way: you develop a development mentality; it is not something you are born with. This is not something that just happens overnight. It's a deliberate choice. You must choose to view the world through the prism of opportunity each and every day when you wake up. You begin to perceive obstacles as stepping stones rather than impenetrable barriers. The true metamorphosis takes place at that change.

You will encounter obstacles. That's a given. The worst part is that setbacks are feedback rather than failures. When you adopt this viewpoint, every challenge turns into a hidden lesson. Did you miss the deadline? Fantastic! What does that teach you? Did a presentation go badly for you? Excellent! Examine it, draw lessons from it, and improve the next time. The cycle of attempting, failing, learning, and trying again is how progress occurs.

Let's dissect this in more detail. The foundation of a growth-oriented attitude is curiosity. You must have a voracious appetite for information. Pose inquiries. Look farther. Never assume anything at face value. Push yourself to extend your views, seek out new experiences, and investigate novel concepts. You start to perceive the world as a playground full with chances to grow and learn as you develop your curiosity.

Imagine that during a meeting, someone brings up a point that you disagree with. The typical individual could completely disregard it. However, you? You're doing more than simply rolling your eyes. "What can I learn from this perspective?" you ask yourself. What aspects of this concept may I use into my own ideas? That is curiosity's power. Disagreements are turned into teaching moments.

Let's now discuss resiliency. A solid foundation is necessary for a development attitude. You must have the willingness to fall and then get back up. Consider all of the prosperous businesspeople you respect. Success wasn't something they waltzed into. They experienced innumerable setbacks, criticism, and rejection. However, they refused to allow such encounters define who they were. They turned them into gasoline. Embracing resilience creates a mental stronghold. You only get stronger with each setback.

And here's a secret: it's crucial to surround oneself with the proper people. "You are the average of the five people you spend the most time with," as the adage goes. It's accurate. Guess what happens if you spend time with doubters and pessimists? That will get ingrained in your thinking. You must surround yourself with individuals who keep you accountable, push you, and encourage you. These are the people that will encourage you to embrace your potential, think beyond the box, and take chances. Locate your tribe and let their positive energy to uplift you.

Let's now explore the power of feedback. For someone with a growth-oriented attitude, feedback is invaluable. You must look for it. Constructive criticism, whether it comes from a mentor, a coworker, or even customers, is extremely beneficial. Accept it instead of running away from it. Express gratitude to those who bring out areas that need improvement! That's a chance to develop. You are not flawless, and that's acceptable. Make use of the feedback to hone your abilities and improve your strategy.

The fascinating part is that a development mentality is characterized by taking chances. You can't progress if you don't take chances. That's how easy it is. However, keep in mind that not all hazards are the same. You must evaluate them. Here's when taking reasonable risks becomes important. A well-considered and well-informed risk has a far higher chance of success. Without a parachute, you don't have to jump into the unknown. Compile your information, weigh your alternatives, and then make the leap.

Let's briefly shift our focus to the idea of flexibility. The planet is undergoing rapid change. You will fall behind if you are set in your ways. Change is welcomed in a growth-oriented attitude. You adapt as fresh knowledge becomes available. When things change, you change course. Your buddy is flexibility. You are flowing, not stiff. You can take advantage of fresh chances and overcome obstacles with agility because to your versatility.

Here's something that may surprise you: it's acceptable to not know everything. The most effective leaders, in actuality, don't act as though they are experts. They acknowledge their knowledge deficiencies and make an effort to close them. This humility creates opportunities for development. It enables you to have meaningful interactions and learn from others. You may unleash your creative and innovative potential when you're receptive to fresh ideas.

You must accept the procedure as well. Success frequently comes after a protracted and convoluted road. The journey itself is more important than the final goal. Honor the little victories. No matter how little a step may appear, it counts as progress. Acknowledging these successes keeps you inspired and strengthens your conviction that you're headed in the right direction. The important thing is that you are gaining momentum.

Now let's discuss the concept of self-compassion. You will make mistakes, and that's okay. Be nice to yourself when you do it. Those with a development mentality recognize that making errors is a necessary part of the process. Consider what went wrong, draw lessons from it, and move on rather than criticizing yourself. Self-compassion like this promotes resilience. It provides a secure environment where you may try new things and take chances without worrying about severe self-judgment.

Not to mention how crucial goal-setting is. You must have attainable objectives that complement your vision. A growth-oriented viewpoint needs guidance. Divide your objectives into doable stages. This framework provides you with a path to follow, which makes it simpler to monitor your development and maintain focus. Your confidence in your capacity to develop is strengthened by each objective you accomplish.

The desire to try new things is another essential component of a development mindset. Don't be scared to take risks. The foundation of invention is experimentation. Be willing to try and fail, whether you're testing a new marketing plan or investigating an alternative company model. Unexpected experiments can lead to some of the most successful discoveries. You won't know if you never try.

Additionally, you ought to cultivate a culture of learning in your surroundings. Create an environment where team members feel free to experiment and share ideas if you're the team leader. Encourage everyone on your team to share their opinions, even if they don't appear conventional. The potential for creativity and teamwork is unlocked when you foster a culture of learning. This environment of progress is advantageous to everybody.

Let's not undervalue the part thankfulness plays in this process. You change your perspective from what you lack to what you have when you approach life with thankfulness. Your development attitude is strengthened by this viewpoint. Instead of focusing on lack, you begin to notice the plenty all around you. Resilience is fostered by an attitude of gratitude. It encourages you to keep going forward and helps you see the lessons you may gain from failures.

Let's now talk about how important it is to act. You are not only a passive spectator if you have a growth-oriented mindset. You take an active part in your path. Thoughts are wonderful, but they are useless if they are not implemented. Make the initial move. Instead than waiting for the ideal moment, make it happen. You get greater confidence the more you act. Every action strengthens the conviction that you can overcome any obstacle.

Additionally, you should regularly reflect. Spend some time evaluating your progress. What have you discovered? What changes have you undergone? This introspection keeps you focused on your own development and helps you stay in line with your objectives. It's a chance to reassess and make any required modifications. Additionally, acknowledging your progress increases your self-esteem and motivates you.

The worst part is that adopting a growth-oriented viewpoint does not guarantee that you won't face difficulties. There will be unexpected turns in life. You will encounter obstacles. However, you change your emphasis when you face such obstacles with a development attitude. Rather of giving up, you start to wonder. The phrase "what can I learn from this?" becomes your guiding principle. You advance because of your interest.

You should look for mentors as well. Look for individuals who have been on the route you wish to go and who encourage you. Gain knowledge from their experiences. Use their knowledge. A mentor may offer priceless advice and insights that will enable you to go through your path with more assurance and clarity. Never undervalue the importance of taking advice from someone who have been there before.

Let's now discuss the significance of honoring intellectual diversity. Be in the company of folks who believe differently than you do. Discuss many points of view. Innovation and creativity are fueled by this diversity of viewpoints. It pushes you to think creatively and consider novel ideas. You broaden your own perspective on the world when you are exposed to many points of view.

In the end, adopting a growth-oriented viewpoint is about taking charge of your story. It's about taking responsibility for your path and creating a fulfilling life. Your world may be shaped by you. Every decision you make and every action you do advances your development.

As you set out on this path, keep in mind that success in terms of money is not the only goal. Being the best version of oneself, learning, and personal development are the main goals. This growth-oriented mentality will lead to the prosperity you desire. You'll discover that life's richness goes beyond numbers when you're committed to growing, learning, and accepting new experiences.

So, go out there. Adopt a growth-oriented mindset. Select activity over passivity, curiosity over complacency, and resilience over loss. It's time for you to make this adventure truly remarkable. The world awaits your realization of your full potential.

Chapter 2
Creating Value in the Marketplace

Identifying Gaps and Opportunities

To put it simply, the foundation of wealth is the creation of value. You must determine where value is missing and fill those gaps if you want to become wealthy enough to begin to wonder what money is all about. It's about changing lives, finding solutions to issues, and actually giving people what they need—not just about earning a quick profit. Money becomes a consequence of your efforts rather than the main objective when you concentrate on creating value.

To begin with, what exactly does the term "creation of value" mean? It's about being aware of the pain points. Examine your surroundings. What kinds of annoyances do people encounter on a daily basis? Which issues are they attempting to resolve? Determine those areas of discomfort and consider ways to ease them. This is about actual people and their hardships, not some abstract idea. You want to be as detailed as possible.

Let's examine how to identify these gaps. Listen first. Engage in conversation. Inquire about their experiences. What would they want to be simpler? What are they sick of enduring? Make use of focus groups, polls, or even informal discussions. The things you discover when you interact with others and pay attention to their opinions will surprise you. This is your treasure trove. These observations serve as the cornerstone upon which your company or product might be constructed.

Analyzing current solutions is the next step after gaining an understanding of the issues individuals encounter. What's available? What is effective? What isn't? This is the environment in which you compete. Expand your horizons and consider more than simply your direct rivals. Think about other options. You can identify shortcomings in the present offers with the use of this study. Determine what is missing. Perhaps it's a better user experience, quality, cost, or accessibility. It is your responsibility to identify that gap and choose how to close it.

Let's be more precise. Consider a typical sector, such as fitness. These days, every single person has a fitness app. However, what is the subject of complaints? These apps are frequently excessively general. They don't accommodate personal preferences. What if you developed a customized fitness software that changes in real time according on user input? There is a gap there! You're giving a customized experience that appeals to people rather than simply another generic answer. That's how true value is created.

Let's also discuss innovation. Value creation is having the guts to challenge the status quo rather than merely making improvements to what currently exists. What can you do differently, ask yourself? What is still unfinished? Examine sectors like healthcare, education, and even real estate that are ready for change. The finest chances are frequently found in fields that appear unchanging or unresponsive. It is you who has the courage to make a difference.

Knowing your audience is another important factor. You're servicing whom? What are their beliefs, goals, and anxieties? This calls for extensive study. Make thorough personalities for your customers. Recognize their choices and reasons. Once your target audience is clearly defined, adjust your offers to suit their requirements. People are more inclined to interact with your product or service when they feel heard and understood.

Now let's turn to the significance of placement. How do you present your offering once a market gap has been identified? This involves creating an engaging story about your goods. Why is it there? What issue does it resolve? What distinguishes it from the competition? Your audience needs to emotionally connect with your messaging. Consumers purchase experiences, tales, and metamorphoses in addition to goods. Make sure that's reflected in your positioning.

Let's now discuss testing your concept. Make a prototype of your idea before investing much. Obtain input often and early. This might entail doing test projects or developing a minimal viable product (MVP). The objective is to validate your idea without investing all of your resources up front. Test your hypotheses and be prepared to change course in response to criticism. This process of iteration is essential. Prior to a complete launch, it enables you to refine your product.

The pricing approach is another important consideration. Even with the greatest product in the world, it won't sell if you set the pricing incorrectly.

Recognize the dynamics of your market. How much would consumers be willing to spend on your solution? Examine the prices of your competitors, but don't just follow their lead. Consider how your pricing is justified by your distinct value offer. You may be shocked at how much people are prepared to pay if you're providing something that actually addresses a problem.

We must not overlook the function of marketing. You must successfully explain the value you have made. Here's where you can use your storytelling skills. To spread the word, use content marketing, email campaigns, and social media. Emphasize the issue you're trying to solve and the advantages of your approach. To establish credibility, use case studies and testimonials. More than anything else, people trust recommendations from their peers. Take advantage of that.

Importantly, you should constantly be prepared to adjust. The market is ever-changing. Technology advances, consumer demands change, and trends change as well. Stay abreast with developments in your field. Ask your consumers for input on a regular basis and keep up with industry advancements. Don't be scared to change course if something isn't working. Your offering will remain valued and relevant with this adaptability.

The significance of creating a community around your business should also be taken into account. Talk to your audience. Develop connections. Customers are more inclined to stick around when they feel like they are a part of something greater. Provide venues for communication, such as forums, social media groups, or events. Promote conversation. Pay attention to what they have to say and include them in your own development.

Let's also discuss scalability. Consider how you may scale your offering as you add value. Is it possible to automate some procedures? Can partnerships or collaborations help you reach a wider audience? Scalability is necessary for long-term expansion. It enables you to have a greater effect without requiring corresponding increases in resources or effort.

You must also know who your competitors are. Pay attention to what other people are doing in order to identify their advantages and disadvantages, not merely to imitate them. Examine their products and client testimonials. Determine the areas in which you can improve. Keep in mind that competition is about identifying and securing your own niche, not just about outperforming others.

Let's adopt a constant improvement attitude. The effort doesn't end when your product is out. Establish systems for continuous feedback. Review your offers on a frequent basis. What do you need to work on? Which characteristics are desired by customers? Your brand remains current and new with this attitude of constant development. It lets your clients know that you respect their experience and are dedicated to providing value.

You should welcome teamwork as well. Partnerships can occasionally be the most effective means of adding value. Determine influencers or businesses that compliment your vision. Working together can help you reach a wider audience and give your clients more value. This is a win-win scenario. Together, you increase your offers, share audiences, and pool resources.

Let's now discuss the long term. Value creation is a marathon, not a sprint. You must be persistent and patient. There will be obstacles in the road, and success takes time. However, the benefits will materialize if you stay committed to adding true value and resolving actual issues. Instead of aiming for a short-term victory, you're laying the groundwork for long-term success.

Additionally, pay attention to the overall state of the economy. Regulations, technological advancements, and shifts in customer behavior can all lead to new possibilities. Remain flexible and receptive. The most successful businesspeople are those who are able to identify trends before they catch on. You can take advantage of new markets and changing customer demands by staying ahead of the curve.

Remembering your brand identity is important. The way you are perceived by others is your brand. Build a powerful, genuine brand that appeals to your target market and embodies your beliefs. Trust is developed via visual identity and message consistency. Consumers who identify with a brand are more likely to support it. Ensure that your brand conveys an engaging narrative that emotionally engages your consumers.

Consider the impact that genuineness may have. Authenticity stands out in a world full with possibilities. Be open and honest about your goal, beliefs, and journey. Tell us about yourself and the motivations behind your offers. Authenticity makes people connect. They are more inclined to support your efforts when they see the true you.

Lastly, never forget the value of giving back. generating a difference is more important than generating money when it comes to creating value. As you mature, consider how you might support issues that are important to you or give back to your community. This builds stronger relationships with your audience in addition to improving the perception of your brand. Supporting companies that are changing the world is something that people adore.

In conclusion, finding opportunities and gaps in the market via careful observation and involvement is the key to adding value. Pay attention to your audience, evaluate current solutions, and take risks with your innovation. Recognize the needs of your audience, properly position your product, and ask for feedback often. Focus on scalability, foster a community, and embrace flexibility. Work along with others, use patience, and always be true to yourself.

You are building a legacy rather than merely pursuing financial gain when you dedicate yourself to producing true worth. Your efforts to help lives and address real issues will lead to your fortune. This is the key to creating a life so wealthy that you begin to wonder what money is all about. Accept this voyage and observe the chances that present themselves. Prepare to innovate, disrupt, and produce value that lasts!

2.1 Leveraging Skills for Profit

Let's get real: the skills you already have can be your ticket to serious wealth. Most people think they need to reinvent the wheel or learn a whole new set of skills to make money. But here's the truth: you're sitting on a goldmine of talent and expertise that, if leveraged properly, can lead you to riches beyond your wildest dreams. So, how do you turn those skills into profit? Buckle up, because we're diving deep.

First off, you need to identify what you're good at. This sounds simple, but a lot of folks overlook it. What comes naturally to you? What do you enjoy doing? Is it writing, graphic design, coding, sales, or even cooking? Take a hard look at your skill set and own it. Make a list. Don't just jot down what you think you should be good at—focus on what you've actually done and what you can do. This is the foundation for your money-making endeavors.

Once you have your skills laid out, it's time to evaluate the market. What are people paying for? Where's the demand? Look at trends in your industry. Dive into online platforms, forums, and social media groups. Pay attention to what people are asking for. What problems are they trying to solve? Align your skills with these demands. This is where the magic happens. You're not just creating something out of thin air; you're offering a solution to a real problem that people are willing to pay for.

Let's say you're a great writer. Instead of just churning out content, think about how you can package that skill. Maybe you create an online course teaching others how to write compelling copy. Or perhaps you offer freelance writing services specifically for businesses looking to enhance their brand voice. The key is to pivot your skill into something that has clear market value. Don't be afraid to think outside the box.

Now, let's talk about niching down. One of the biggest mistakes people make is trying to appeal to everyone. Stop that. It's a recipe for mediocrity. Instead, identify a niche where you can shine. For instance, if you're a graphic designer, don't just say you can design anything. Instead, focus on creating infographics for the health and wellness industry. This not only sets you apart but makes it easier for potential clients to see the value in what you offer. When you specialize, you become the go-to expert, and that's where you can charge premium rates.

When you've nailed down your niche, it's time to showcase your skills. This is all about building credibility. Create a portfolio that highlights your best work. If you're a designer, put together a sleek website with your top projects. If you're a writer, compile samples that showcase your versatility. Use testimonials from previous clients to bolster your credibility. Social proof is everything. When potential customers see that others have had positive experiences with you, they're much more likely to trust you.

But let's be clear: just having a great portfolio isn't enough. You need to market yourself. Start by leveraging social media. Create content that showcases your expertise. Share tips, insights, and behind-the-scenes looks at your work. Use platforms like LinkedIn, Instagram, or TikTok to engage with your audience. The more you share, the more visibility you gain. People want to work with those who not only excel at their craft but are also approachable and relatable.

Now, let's talk about monetization strategies. There are countless ways to profit from your skills. You can offer one-on-one coaching or consulting. This is a great way to leverage your expertise directly and provide value while charging a premium for your time. You could also create digital products like e-books or online courses. Once you build them, they can generate passive income for you.

Consider membership sites or subscription models, too. If you can provide ongoing value—whether through exclusive content, community support, or regular updates—people will pay for that access. This is where you can create a steady stream of income without constantly trading time for money.

Let's not forget about freelancing. It's a great way to jump in without a huge commitment. Platforms like Upwork or Fiverr can help you find clients looking for your specific skills. You can start small, build your reputation, and scale up from there. Once you establish a client base, you can raise your rates. And trust me, clients are willing to pay for quality work. Don't undersell yourself.

Now, if you want to take it a step further, think about collaborating with others. Find people who have complementary skills. For example, if you're a marketer, partner with a web developer to offer a complete package for businesses. By combining forces, you can tap into each other's networks, expand your reach, and create more value together. This strategy can open doors you didn't even know existed.

As you're building your skill-based business, you need to stay relevant. Industries change, and new skills become essential. Keep learning. Invest in yourself. Whether it's taking courses, attending workshops, or simply reading industry-related content, continuous learning is crucial. The more you know, the more valuable you become.

And let's not forget about networking. Your network is your net worth. Build relationships with other professionals in your field. Attend events, join industry groups, and engage with others online. The connections you make can lead to new opportunities, partnerships, and even clients. Be genuine in your interactions. You're not just looking for what you can get; you're building relationships that can foster growth for everyone involved.

Now, let's dive into the mindset of abundance. When you're leveraging your skills for profit, it's easy to fall into a scarcity mindset. You might think, "What if I don't find clients?" or "What if someone else is better than me?" Shift that narrative. Focus on the value you bring. Your unique perspective, your experiences—no one else has those. Believe in your abilities and your worth. The market is vast, and there's plenty of room for everyone.

And remember, feedback is your friend. When you start putting your skills out there, seek feedback from clients and peers. It might sting a little, but it's invaluable. Use that feedback to refine your offerings and improve your services. Continuous improvement is a hallmark of success.

Let's talk about pricing strategies. When you start charging for your services, it can be daunting. What do you charge? Look at industry standards, but don't feel constrained by them. Value your time and expertise. If you're delivering exceptional results, don't be afraid to set premium prices. It's about the value you provide, not just the time you spend. If someone is getting a return on investment from your work, they'll gladly pay for it.

Also, consider creating package deals or bundled services. This can add value for your clients while increasing your revenue per transaction. For example, if you offer social media management, consider bundling content creation, strategy sessions, and analytics reviews into one comprehensive package. This not only streamlines your offerings but also makes it easier for clients to see the value.

As you grow, consider scalability. How can you turn your skills into a business that doesn't rely solely on your time? Think about systems, processes, and team building. Can you automate parts of your service? Can you hire freelancers or contractors to handle overflow work? The goal is to create a business model that allows you to expand without sacrificing quality.

Let's address the elephant in the room: fear of failure. It's real, and it can be paralyzing. But here's the deal: every successful person has faced failure. It's part of the process. Embrace it. Use failures as learning opportunities. Analyze what went wrong and adapt. The most successful people are those who keep pushing forward, despite the setbacks.

Lastly, make sure you're tracking your progress. Set clear goals for what you want to achieve. Monitor your income, client acquisition, and overall growth. This not only helps you stay accountable but also provides valuable insights into what's working and what isn't.

In summary, leveraging your skills for profit is about recognizing the value you already possess. Identify your strengths, align them with market demands, and niche down. Showcase your skills effectively and market yourself relentlessly. Explore various monetization strategies, whether through freelancing, coaching, or digital products. Collaborate with others, invest in continuous learning, and build a strong network.

Adopt an abundance mindset, value your worth, and embrace feedback. Price your services appropriately, create scalable offerings, and don't let fear hold you back. Track your progress and adapt as needed. By following these steps, you'll turn your skills into a profitable venture that not only generates income but also creates lasting impact.

Now go out there, take action, and start leveraging your skills. The world is waiting for what you have to offer. You've got this!

2.2 Innovating for Long-Term Success

Alright, let's dive into the nitty-gritty of innovation. If you want to achieve long-term success and get so rich you start questioning the meaning of money, you need to understand that innovation is not just a buzzword; it's a survival skill. In today's fast-paced world, businesses that don't innovate are like dinosaurs—eventually, they go extinct. So, how do you harness innovation to not just survive, but thrive? Buckle up.

First things first, innovation starts with a mindset. You have to cultivate a culture of curiosity. Ask questions. Challenge the status quo. When you're running a business, it's easy to get comfortable and stick to what works. But let me tell you, comfort zones are where great ideas go to die. Foster an environment where questioning is encouraged. Your team should feel empowered to bring new ideas to the table without the fear of being shot down. Create a space where experimentation is the norm, not the exception.

Now, let's address a common misconception: innovation isn't just for tech companies. Sure, the Silicon Valley startups have their flashy apps and cutting-edge technologies, but innovation can happen in any industry. Whether you're in retail, healthcare, or education, there are always ways to innovate your processes, services, and customer experiences. Don't limit yourself to what's expected in your field. Break the mold.

A crucial part of this innovation mindset is being open to feedback. Your customers are your best source of insight. They're the ones using your product or service, and their experiences will give you a clear picture of what's working and what's not. Don't just ask for feedback when things go wrong. Make it a regular practice. Use surveys, focus groups, or just casual conversations. The more you listen, the more opportunities for innovation will reveal themselves.

Let's get specific. Look for areas where you can improve efficiency. Can your processes be streamlined? Are there bottlenecks that frustrate your team or your customers? Identify them. For instance, if you're running an e-commerce site and customers frequently abandon their carts, dig into why that's happening. Is the checkout process too complicated? Is shipping too slow? Tackle those issues head-on. Innovations that simplify the user experience often lead to increased sales and customer satisfaction.

Next, let's talk about technology. It's evolving at lightning speed, and if you're not leveraging the latest tools, you're falling behind. Invest in technology that aligns with your business goals. This could mean adopting new software for project management, utilizing AI for customer service, or even incorporating data analytics to make informed decisions. The right technology can be a game-changer, allowing you to operate more efficiently and make smarter choices.

Another critical aspect of innovation is diversification. Don't put all your eggs in one basket. Explore new products, services, or markets. This doesn't mean you should abandon your core offerings; instead, think of it as a way to complement what you already have. For example, if you run a gym, consider offering nutrition coaching or online fitness classes. This not only brings in additional revenue streams but also enhances the overall value you provide to your customers.

Part of diversification is understanding trends in the marketplace. Stay ahead of the curve. What are the emerging trends in your industry? What are consumers increasingly interested in? For instance, sustainability has become a major focus for consumers. If you're in manufacturing, how can you innovate to reduce your carbon footprint? Not only does this align with consumer values, but it can also set you apart from competitors who are lagging behind.

Let's not forget about collaboration. Partnering with other businesses can lead to innovative solutions that you might not come up with on your own. Look for companies with complementary strengths. Together, you can combine resources, share knowledge, and create something unique that neither of you could achieve independently. This could be as simple as co-hosting a webinar or as complex as developing a joint product line. The key is to create a win-win scenario.

Innovation also requires a certain level of risk-taking. You can't be afraid to fail. Every successful entrepreneur has a long list of failures that led to their ultimate success. Don't shy away from trying new things just because they might not work out. It's a learning process. Analyze what didn't work and pivot accordingly. Remember, the greatest innovations often come from trial and error.

Let's talk about measuring success. Once you've implemented innovative strategies, how do you know if they're working? Set clear metrics to track your progress. This could be sales figures, customer satisfaction scores, or engagement metrics. Regularly review these numbers to see what's working and what needs adjustment. If something isn't yielding the results you anticipated, don't be afraid to scrap it and try something new.

Innovation isn't a one-time event; it's an ongoing journey. To stay competitive, you must commit to continuous improvement. Regularly assess your processes, products, and services. Stay curious and always be on the lookout for ways to enhance your offerings. This proactive approach will keep you ahead of the competition and ensure that you're always meeting the evolving needs of your customers.

Let's not forget about the power of storytelling. When you innovate, tell the story behind it. Why did you make that change? What problem does it solve? Share your journey with your customers. When they understand the "why" behind your innovations, they're more likely to resonate with your brand and become loyal advocates. People connect with stories; make sure yours is compelling.

And speaking of loyalty, innovation can also enhance customer retention. When customers see that you're consistently improving and adapting to their needs, they're more likely to stick around. Loyalty programs, exclusive content, or personalized experiences can be powerful tools for fostering a loyal customer base. Remember, retaining existing customers is often more cost-effective than acquiring new ones.

Let's talk about the importance of staying adaptable. The business landscape is constantly changing. What worked yesterday might not work today. Be prepared to pivot your strategies and adjust to new circumstances. This adaptability is key to long-term success. It signals to your customers that you're not just in it for the short haul; you're committed to meeting their needs now and in the future.

As you innovate, keep your eye on your brand identity. Your innovations should align with your core values and mission. Don't chase trends just for the sake of it. Ensure that every new product or service reflects what you stand for as a company. This consistency builds trust with your customers. They'll know what to expect from you, and that predictability can enhance their loyalty.

Let's not ignore the competitive landscape. Keep an eye on your competitors. What are they doing that's innovative? What can you learn from them? This doesn't mean you should copy them; rather, use their successes and failures as a learning opportunity. Understand how you can differentiate yourself and offer something that truly stands out.

And here's a reality check: not every innovation will be a home run. Some will flop, and that's okay. Embrace it. Analyze the failure and learn from it. If you can cultivate a culture where failure is seen as a stepping stone to success, you'll foster an environment ripe for innovation. Encourage your team to take calculated risks and support them when things don't go as planned.

Let's talk about funding innovation. Sometimes, you'll need capital to pursue your innovative ideas. This could mean reinvesting profits, seeking out investors, or even applying for grants. Have a solid plan in place. Show potential investors the value of your innovation. Demonstrate how it will benefit your business and the market at large. Convince them that your idea is worth their investment.

And don't forget about your team. Innovation isn't a solo endeavor. Foster a collaborative environment where everyone feels empowered to contribute. Hold brainstorming sessions, hackathons, or innovation challenges. Encourage your team to share their ideas. You'll be surprised at the gems that can come from your staff. Everyone brings unique perspectives, and tapping into that can lead to some incredible breakthroughs.

Let's circle back to the customer. They should always be at the center of your innovation efforts. Regularly engage with them to understand their evolving needs and preferences. Create feedback loops that allow you to hear directly from your audience. This can include surveys, focus groups, or even casual chats. The more you involve your customers in the process, the more likely you are to create something they'll love.

Finally, remember that the road to innovation can be bumpy. There will be challenges, setbacks, and obstacles. Stay resilient. Keep pushing forward. Every obstacle is an opportunity in disguise. Learn from them, adapt, and keep your eyes on the prize. The journey might be tough, but the rewards—both financial and personal—will be worth it.

In conclusion, innovating for long-term success is about fostering a culture of curiosity, embracing feedback, and continuously seeking improvement. Don't be afraid to take risks, learn from failures, and adapt your strategies as needed. Collaborate with others, stay on top of industry trends, and always keep your customers at the heart of your innovation efforts.

By committing to this mindset and approach, you won't just build a successful business—you'll create a legacy. A legacy that goes beyond wealth and makes a meaningful impact in the lives of others. So get out there, start innovating, and watch how it transforms your journey toward questioning the very meaning of money. You've got this!

Chapter 3
Scaling Your Income Streams

Diversifying Your Revenue Channels

Let's get right to the point: diversifying your sources of income is essential if you want to truly become wealthy. It's like walking a tightrope without a net when you only have one source of income. You could end up in a world of pain with only one mistake. So, how can you generate several revenue streams and expand your income? Hold on tight, because we are going to go over the entire playbook.

Let's start by discussing what diversification entails. Creating a strong financial ecosystem is more important than simply having several streams. Interdependent channels that can help one another are what you want to establish. One stream may flood in as another ebbs. You want a little bit of everything to keep your plate full, so think of it as a financial buffet.

Make use of what you already have first. Examine what you have to give now. What are you doing now that you could do more of? Think about including related services if your company is service-based. Suppose you work as a personal trainer. Why not provide dietary guidance? Alternatively, if you work as a consultant, compile your knowledge into an online course. These extra services have the potential to draw in new clients while also benefiting current ones.

Let's talk about passive income next. This is the ultimate goal of accumulating riches. Suppose you could earn money while you slept. It sounds fantastic, doesn't it? To get there, consider developing goods that will eventually bring in money. These might be subscription services, online courses, or e-books. These goods can generate revenue with little more effort once you make the initial investment. By doing this, you may make the most of your time and increase your earning potential.

Suppose you make the decision to develop an online course. Choose a subject that you are knowledgeable and enthusiastic about first. What is the most common question people ask you? What information do you have that might be useful to others? After you've identified it, plan your route. Take the time to produce excellent material. Delivering genuine value is more important than simply putting up a few videos.

It's time to start marketing your course once it's available. To spread the word, use email lists, social media, and even sponsored advertisements. Don't be afraid to display testimonials. Prospective students are far more inclined to enroll in your course when they realize that others have found it beneficial.

Let's now turn our attention to affiliate marketing. Think about marketing goods or services you support if you already have a platform, such as a blog, YouTube channel, or social media presence. You may make commissions here without having to start from scratch. Select affiliates who complement your brand and benefit your readers.

Authenticity is essential to affiliate marketing success. Don't just advertise anything to get money. Your audience has faith in you. Retain that trust by only endorsing goods that you truly believe in. Your audience is more inclined to follow your advice when you are open and honest.

Digitized items are another effective avenue. The need for online materials is growing rapidly in our digital age. If you can produce software, instructions, or templates that help your audience solve an issue, you've struck gold. One of the best things about digital products is their cheap overhead. You make it once and then sell it again and again.

Think about the abilities you possess that may be used to create a digital product. Do you have exceptional graphic design skills? Make templates for corporate presentations or social media postings. Why not create e-books or manuals if you are an accomplished writer? There are countless alternatives. Just keep in mind that you should concentrate on resolving a particular issue for your audience. The true value is found there.

The topic of investing will now be discussed. You must make your money work for you if you wish to increase your revenue. Knowing the fundamentals of investing is essential, but it doesn't mean you have to become a financial whiz overnight. Invest in things that will increase in value over time, such as stocks, real estate, or launching a side company.

One of the best ways to diversify your income is through real estate. The value of rental properties usually rises over time, and they can offer a consistent income flow. Investigate. Recognize the market. Seek for real estate in regions that have development potential. You want to be sure that your investment will eventually pay for itself.

Not to be overlooked is the strength of community building. Building a community around your business, whether through a newsletter, membership website, or social media group, may provide a steady flow of revenue. Fees for special content or subscriptions. Access to a community where they may grow, learn, and meet like-minded people is something that people are prepared to pay for.

In relation to community, think of holding seminars or events. This might take place in person or virtually. Communicate your knowledge and establish a stronger connection with your audience. Don't be scared to charge for entry and provide high-end experiences. Attendees would gladly pay for the chance to learn from you if you provide value.

Let's change topics and discuss coaching or consulting. Think about becoming a consultant if you've established a solid reputation in your industry. Companies are constantly searching for specialists to assist them in resolving issues. Package your expertise into consulting or coaching services. You can demand higher prices, particularly if you've become recognized as an expert in your field.

You could now be concerned about the time commitment. It's true that it takes work to scale your revenue sources. However, consider this: every new stream you generate can ultimately run automatically. After creating a community, affiliate links, or a course, the revenue may be generated with little further work. In the long term, your early time and effort commitment is worthwhile.

Let's discuss cooperation. One effective strategy to diversify your revenue is to collaborate with other business owners. Seek for companies or people in your niche that compliment each other. Working together allows you to share audiences, pool resources, and develop collaborative products. This might be a shared membership website, a co-branded product, or even a webinar. Working together broadens your audience and generates other revenue streams.

Keep in mind that not every source of revenue needs to be a game-changing concept. Occasionally, little adjustments can have a significant impact. Seek methods to make money off of your current resources or abilities. If you're a photographer, you might want to sell your photographs as stock photography.

Make prints or other items that showcase your artwork if you're an artist. Over time, these little streams might accumulate.

Let's now discuss the significance of automating your revenue sources. After you've created a number of revenue streams, try to find methods to make procedures more efficient. Make use of software and technologies that may assist you in automating processes such as sales funnels, customer support, and email marketing. You can devote more time to expanding your business if you spend less time on monotonous duties.

To handle your prospects and clients, think about putting in place a CRM system. This enables you to keep your audience interested and build relationships with them. You may also find possible upsell chances with the aid of a well-structured system. Understanding the demands of your clients will enable you to provide value and boost sales.

Let's talk about the worry of overcommitting. It's a legitimate worry, but setting priorities is crucial. Pay attention to the sources of income that complement your interests and strong points. Don't feel pressured to do everything at once. Begin modestly. Proceed to the next stream as soon as the first one is operational.

Diversification has the advantage of providing a safety net. You will have alternative streams to rely on in case one has difficulties. Long-term success depends on this resiliency. You may take measured risks without worrying about total financial loss since it gives you piece of mind.

Let's return to the significance of client connections now. Keep the individuals who make the purchases in mind as you grow your revenue sources. Regularly interact with your audience. Get their opinion. What are they seeking? What difficulties do they face? Make changes to your offers based on this input.

Your several revenue streams are more likely to be supported by an active audience. Whether you suggest a new product or service, they will believe it. Establish that connection. Express your sincere concern for their needs. The likelihood that they will invest in what you have to offer increases with the strength of the relationship.

Not to be overlooked is personal branding. Your brand becomes increasingly more important as you expand. Make sure that all of your channels convey the same message. Keep your brand voice and identity consistent across all platforms, including your website, social media accounts, and email newsletters. This constancy fosters trust and recognition.

Develop the practice of routinely reviewing your revenue sources as you grow. What is effective? What isn't? To monitor your performance, use analytics. Do not be afraid to change course or shut down a channel if it is not producing the anticipated profits. Your resources and time are precious; concentrate on what will yield the greatest outcomes.

Last but not least, keep in mind that wealth is more than simply money. It all comes down to the influence and way of life you wish to establish. In addition to ensuring financial independence, income diversification creates additional opportunities for personal development and enjoyment. Consider what you genuinely hope to accomplish. What would you like to do with your time? What kind of legacy would you like to leave?

To sum up, diversifying your sources of income is crucial to accumulating long-term wealth. Leverage investments, investigate digital goods, generate passive income, and start with what you currently have. Create a community, provide advisory services, and think about working together. Put client connections first and automate procedures.

By employing these tactics, you're constructing a robust and lasting financial future rather than only generating revenue. This is how you become so wealthy that you begin to wonder what money is all about. So, go out there, do something, and begin expanding your sources of income. The moment to take action is now, and the prospects are limitless!

3.1 Automating for Efficiency

Alright, let's dive into automation—one of the most crucial elements for scaling your business and maximizing your income. If you want to get so rich you start questioning the meaning of money, you need to think like a machine. Not in a soulless way, but in a smart, efficient way. Automation is about freeing up your time so you can focus on what really matters—growing your business and creating value.

First off, what exactly do I mean by automation? Simply put, it's about taking repetitive tasks off your plate and letting technology handle them. You can't afford to be stuck in the weeds, doing the same mundane tasks day in and day out. If you're spending hours on tasks that don't move the needle, you're losing out on opportunities. Think about it: what tasks consume your time that could be automated? Email responses, invoicing, social media posting? All of these are prime candidates for automation.

Let's kick things off with email automation. If you're not using email marketing to engage with your audience, you're missing out. But sending individual emails to every person on your list? That's a huge waste of time. Use email marketing software to automate your campaigns. Set up welcome sequences for new subscribers, send follow-ups, or even automate your sales funnels. This way, you're nurturing your leads without lifting a finger.

Imagine this: you launch a new product. You send an automated email to your list announcing it. That email goes out while you're busy doing something else. You don't even have to think about it. As your list grows, so does your reach. More emails mean more engagement, and more engagement means more sales. The beauty of this is that you can be doing other things—working on your next big idea or spending time with your family—while your email campaigns run themselves.

Now, let's move on to customer relationship management (CRM) systems. If you're not using a CRM, you're seriously missing the boat. A good CRM organizes your contacts, tracks interactions, and helps you manage your leads and customers more effectively. Automate your follow-ups. Schedule reminders to check in on potential clients. Create automated workflows that trigger actions based on customer behavior. For example, if a lead downloads a free resource, have an automated email sequence set up to nurture them into a paying customer.

This isn't just about saving time; it's about building relationships at scale. You can engage with hundreds or even thousands of potential customers, all while maintaining a personal touch. People appreciate when you remember their names, their needs, and their past interactions. Automation allows you to do that without becoming a robot.

Let's talk about invoicing and payments. If you're still sending invoices manually, you need to step up your game. Use software to automate your billing process. This not only saves you time but also minimizes errors. You send an invoice, it gets paid automatically, and you don't have to worry about chasing down payments. This is crucial for cash flow. When you automate invoicing, you ensure that money flows into your business consistently.

And don't just stop at invoicing. Set up recurring billing for services. If you're running a subscription-based business, automate those payments. This way, you can rely on predictable income each month. You're not left wondering if clients will pay on time; the system handles it for you. That reliability lets you plan better and grow your business more confidently.

Now, let's discuss social media automation. If you're spending hours every week posting on social media, it's time to rethink your strategy. Use tools to schedule your posts in advance. This allows you to create a month's worth of content in one sitting and let the software do the heavy lifting. You can focus on engagement and creating great content rather than stressing over daily posts.

But scheduling is just the beginning. Look for tools that help you analyze your social media performance. Which posts are getting the most engagement? What times are your followers most active? Use that data to inform your strategy. The more you know about your audience, the better you can serve them. Automation helps you gather insights without having to manually track everything.

Let's pivot to your website. If you don't have automation set up on your site, you're leaving money on the table. Use chatbots to handle common customer inquiries. You can provide instant support without being available 24/7. This not only enhances customer satisfaction but also frees you up to focus on more complex issues. Chatbots can answer questions about your services, direct users to relevant resources, and even help with lead generation.

Consider setting up an FAQ page or resources section on your site that automates responses to common questions. If potential customers can find the answers they need without having to reach out to you, they're more likely to convert. It's all about making the customer journey as seamless as possible.

Now, let's talk about content creation. I know, this is where things can get messy. You might think, "Alex, I can't automate creativity!" True, but you can streamline your content processes. Create templates for your blogs, social media posts, and videos. Establish a content calendar so you know what to create and when. This keeps you organized and efficient.

You can even use AI tools to help generate ideas or draft content. While it might not be perfect, it can give you a starting point that you can refine. The goal isn't to eliminate creativity; it's to free up mental space so you can focus on high-impact tasks. When you automate the mundane, you're left with more energy for innovation.

Let's shift gears and discuss team communication. If you have a team, consider using project management tools to automate workflows. These platforms allow you to set deadlines, assign tasks, and track progress all in one place. Automate reminders for deadlines and status updates. This keeps everyone accountable without constant check-ins.

And let's be honest: the less time you spend managing the day-to-day, the more time you can devote to strategic growth. Create a culture of accountability where team members take ownership of their tasks. Automate where you can to minimize micromanagement. This not only empowers your team but also boosts morale. Everyone loves when their time is respected.

Now, here's something that often gets overlooked: feedback loops. Automation can play a crucial role in gathering customer feedback. Use surveys or feedback forms that automatically send out after a purchase or service interaction. Analyze this data regularly. What are your customers saying? What do they love? What do they want to see improved? Use automation to ensure you're always in tune with your audience's needs.

Implementing feedback loops also helps you iterate on your offerings. When you know what your customers want, you can adjust your services or products to meet those demands. This is how you create a customer-centric business. They feel valued, and you stay relevant. It's a win-win.

Now, let's talk about scaling. As your business grows, the tasks that once felt manageable can become overwhelming. Automation is the key to scaling efficiently. When you have multiple income streams, the last thing you want is to get bogged down in administrative tasks. By automating processes, you can scale your business without sacrificing your time or sanity.

Think about your future. Do you want to be tied to your desk, constantly working? Or do you want to build a business that runs itself? By investing in automation now, you set the stage for long-term growth. You create a system that can adapt and expand as your business evolves.

And let's face it—automation isn't just about efficiency; it's about creating freedom. The more you automate, the more time you have to focus on what truly matters: innovation, strategy, and building relationships. You can spend your time brainstorming new ideas, developing partnerships, or even just enjoying life outside of work.

Let's wrap this up by addressing a common fear: "What if I lose the personal touch?" Automation doesn't mean you lose that connection with your customers. It's about enhancing it. Use automation to handle the repetitive stuff, and then spend the time you save on meaningful interactions. Personalize your communication when it matters. A handwritten note or a personal email goes a long way in building relationships.

In conclusion, automating for efficiency is not just a nice-to-have; it's a must-have if you want to create real wealth. Look for repetitive tasks that can be automated. Invest in tools that streamline your processes. Use automation to enhance customer relationships, manage your team, and gather valuable feedback.

By implementing these strategies, you set yourself up for success. You're not just working harder; you're working smarter. And that's the key to getting so rich you start questioning the very meaning of money. So go out there, start automating, and watch your business thrive!

3.2 Investing in Passive Income Opportunities

Let's cut to the chase: if you want to build real wealth, you've got to get serious about passive income. You've probably heard the term thrown around, but what does it really mean? Passive income is about creating revenue streams that flow into your bank account even when you're not actively working. Imagine making money while you sleep. Sounds good, right? But how do you actually get there? That's what we're going to unpack.

First, let's look at the mindset shift you need. Passive income isn't about luck or getting rich quick. It's about making smart investments in systems that pay off over time. You need to think long-term. Get comfortable with the idea that some investments might take time to yield results. You want to plant seeds now for a harvest later. If you can embrace that mindset, you're already ahead of the game.

Let's dive into some classic passive income opportunities, starting with real estate. Real estate is one of the most popular and effective ways to generate passive income. You buy a property, rent it out, and boom—money flows in every month. But let's be real: it's not as simple as just buying a house. You've got to do your homework.

First, research the market. Look for areas that are on the rise. You want to invest in properties that are going to appreciate in value over time. Find neighborhoods with good schools, amenities, and low crime rates. That's where people want to live. And if you can find a property that's undervalued, even better. This is where you can create instant equity and set yourself up for future gains.

Next, consider what type of property you want to invest in. Are you thinking single-family homes, multi-family units, or maybe commercial properties? Each has its pros and cons. Single-family homes might be easier to manage, but multi-family units can provide multiple streams of income from one location. And commercial properties often come with longer leases and higher returns, but they can be a bit more complex to manage. Decide what aligns with your goals and risk tolerance.

Once you've got your property, you need to find tenants. This is where property management comes into play. If you want truly passive income, you might want to hire a property management company. They handle everything from tenant screening to maintenance. Sure, there's a cost involved, but think of it as an investment in your freedom. You want to be able to enjoy the fruits of your labor without being bogged down by day-to-day management tasks.

Let's move into the realm of dividend stocks. Investing in dividend-paying stocks is another excellent way to generate passive income. Companies that pay dividends are typically more established and financially stable. They reward their shareholders for holding onto their stock by distributing a portion of their earnings.

Research is key here too. Look for companies with a strong history of dividend payments. You want to find those that not only pay dividends but also increase them over time. Reinvest those dividends, and you're setting yourself up for exponential growth. This is the snowball effect at work. The more you invest, the more you earn, and the cycle continues.

Consider creating a diversified portfolio. Don't just put all your eggs in one basket. Mix it up with a combination of growth stocks, value stocks, and, of course, dividend stocks. This approach reduces risk and helps stabilize your income. Plus, with platforms available today, you can easily buy fractional shares, making it accessible even if you're starting small.

Now, let's talk about digital products. Creating digital products can generate passive income with relatively low overhead. Think e-books, online courses, or software. Once you create a high-quality product, you can sell it repeatedly without additional costs. It's the ultimate way to leverage your knowledge and skills.

Identify a niche where you have expertise and can add value. If you're a fitness expert, create a workout program or nutrition guide. If you're a financial whiz, consider an online course on budgeting or investing. The beauty of digital products is that you can market them globally. Your reach isn't limited by geography, and that opens up endless possibilities for income.

Once your product is created, you can automate sales through an online platform. Set up a website, implement a sales funnel, and use email marketing to promote your product. This way, you can generate sales around the clock. You'll need to put in the work upfront, but once it's established, it can operate without your constant involvement.

Let's not overlook peer-to-peer lending. This is where you lend your money to individuals or small businesses through online platforms, earning interest on your investment. It's like being your own bank. Just like any investment, it comes with risks, so you need to do your due diligence. Assess the borrowers and understand the platform's track record before jumping in.

Consider diversifying your lending portfolio. Don't put all your money into one loan. Spread it across multiple borrowers to mitigate risk. The returns can be attractive, especially if you're willing to take on some risk for higher yields. But remember, always evaluate the potential downsides.

Next, let's explore the world of affiliate marketing. If you have a blog, website, or social media following, you can monetize that audience through affiliate partnerships. Promote products or services you believe in and earn a commission on each sale made through your unique link. This is a great way to generate income without having to create a product yourself.

Choose products that align with your brand and that your audience would find valuable. Authenticity is key. Your audience trusts your recommendations, so don't promote anything just for the sake of a paycheck. Build genuine partnerships with brands you believe in, and your followers will appreciate it.

Now, let's talk about creating a membership site. This is where you provide exclusive content or resources to paying members. It could be anything from in-depth training videos, community forums, or downloadable resources. This is a great way to build a recurring income stream.

Consider the type of content you can offer. What problems are you solving for your audience? What can you provide that they can't easily find elsewhere? The key is to create a valuable community that people are willing to pay to be a part of. You can use platforms like Patreon or Teachable to set up your membership site easily.

Let's touch on the world of royalties. If you're a creative person—think musicians, writers, or artists—consider how you can earn passive income through royalties. Create a song, write a book, or produce artwork, and every time someone purchases or uses your creation, you earn a royalty. This is money that keeps coming in without ongoing effort on your part.

Now, let's think about the long game. Passive income opportunities often require an upfront investment of time, money, or both. You might need to spend time creating a product, researching stocks, or hunting for real estate deals. But the goal is to set things up in such a way that you can eventually step back and let the money flow in.

One common mistake people make is expecting passive income to be truly hands-off right away. It's like planting a tree. You need to nurture it before it bears fruit. That initial investment is crucial. You're not just going to wake up one day with a thriving passive income stream without putting in the work first.

Let's pivot to investing in index funds. If you want a simple, effective way to earn passive income, consider index funds. They offer diversification, lower fees, and historically have outperformed most actively managed funds over the long haul. You put your money in, and it grows over time without the need for constant management.

Investing in index funds is about the long game. You're not trying to time the market; you're riding the wave. Set it, forget it, and watch it grow. This is a fantastic way to build wealth without the stress of picking individual stocks.

Now, let's talk about the importance of tracking your passive income. You've got to know where your money is coming from. Use tools and software to track your investments, income streams, and expenses. This will give you a clear picture of how your passive income is performing.

Regularly assess your income streams. What's working? What's not? Use this information to make adjustments. Maybe it's time to invest more in what's performing well or cut loose what's dragging you down. Being proactive will help you maximize your earnings and grow your wealth.

Finally, let's discuss the power of mindset in building passive income. You need to embrace a mindset of abundance. Don't let fear or doubt hold you back from taking calculated risks. Building passive income streams is about making informed decisions, not being paralyzed by what-ifs.

Surround yourself with people who understand the journey you're on. Join communities or networks focused on investing and entrepreneurship. Share your experiences, learn from others, and stay motivated. This is crucial for keeping that momentum going.

In conclusion, investing in passive income opportunities is one of the smartest moves you can make on your wealth-building journey. Real estate, dividend stocks, digital products, peer-to-peer lending, affiliate marketing, membership sites, and royalties are all paths you can explore.

Understand that it's a long-term game. You need to invest time and effort upfront. Track your income streams, stay informed, and adjust as needed. Embrace the mindset of abundance and take calculated risks. This is how you build a financial future that allows you to get so rich you start questioning the meaning of money. So get out there and start creating those passive income streams. The opportunity is waiting for you!

Chapter 4
Building a Resilient Business

Crafting a Sustainable Business Model

Let's get real about what it takes to build a business that not only survives but thrives in today's fast-paced, ever-changing landscape. We're talking about resilience, and that starts with crafting a sustainable business model. If you want to get so rich you start questioning the meaning of money, you've got to build a foundation that can withstand the storms.

First off, what does it mean to have a sustainable business model? It's about creating a structure that not only generates revenue but does so in a way that can adapt to change. You want to ensure that your business can pivot when necessary, respond to market demands, and weather economic downturns without crumbling. It's not just about making a quick buck; it's about building something that lasts.

Let's start with understanding your value proposition. This is your promise to your customers—the unique value you provide that sets you apart from the competition. It's the reason they choose you over everyone else. You've got to nail this down before you can build anything else. Spend time figuring out what makes your offering irresistible. Is it the quality, the price, the service? Identify that key element and leverage it in every aspect of your business.

Once you have your value proposition, it's time to define your target market. Who are you serving? Get granular here. Understand their pain points, desires, and behaviors. This isn't just about demographics; it's about psychographics. What drives them? What keeps them up at night? The more you know about your audience, the better you can tailor your offerings to meet their needs.

Now, let's talk revenue streams. Diversification is key. Relying on a single source of income is a recipe for disaster. Explore multiple revenue channels. If you're selling a product, consider adding complementary services. If you're offering a service, think about creating related products. This not only stabilizes your income but also opens up new opportunities for growth.

Consider subscription models. They provide predictable revenue and foster customer loyalty. Whether it's a monthly box, a membership site, or a service that charges a recurring fee, subscriptions can create a steady cash flow. This model allows you to build deeper relationships with your customers over time, and that's where the magic happens.

Next, let's dive into your cost structure. Understanding your costs is crucial for sustainability. You need to know where your money is going. Fixed costs, variable costs—get granular with your budget. Identify areas where you can cut costs without sacrificing quality. The goal is to maximize your profit margins while delivering value.

Think about your supply chain. Are there ways to optimize it? Can you negotiate better rates with suppliers? Streamlining your operations not only cuts costs but also increases efficiency. And that efficiency translates into better service for your customers.

Now, let's discuss scalability. Your business model should be designed for growth. This means you need systems in place that can handle increased demand without breaking a sweat. Whether it's automating processes or leveraging technology, make sure your operations can scale seamlessly. You don't want to be in a position where you're turning away business because you can't handle the workload.

As you build your business, always keep an eye on the competition. This doesn't mean you need to copy them; rather, you should be aware of what's working in the market and what's not. Regularly assess your competitors' strengths and weaknesses. Use this information to refine your own strategies. What can you do better? What gaps can you fill? Staying informed keeps you agile and helps you stay one step ahead.

Let's talk about customer feedback. If you're not actively seeking feedback, you're missing a golden opportunity. Your customers hold the keys to your success. Implement systems to gather their opinions, suggestions, and concerns. This could be through surveys, social media, or direct communication. Use that data to make informed decisions. When you listen to your customers, you build loyalty and trust.

Now, let's get into marketing. You can have the best product in the world, but if nobody knows about it, you're not going to make any sales. Develop a marketing strategy that aligns with your business model. Utilize a mix of channels—social media, email marketing, content marketing, and paid ads. The key is to create consistent messaging that resonates with your target audience.

Don't overlook the power of storytelling. People connect with stories. Share your brand's journey, your values, and the impact you're making. Authenticity breeds trust. When your audience feels connected to your story, they're more likely to support your business.

Now, let's pivot to building a strong brand. Your brand is more than just a logo; it's your reputation. Invest time in developing a brand that reflects your values and resonates with your audience. Consistency is crucial—make sure your messaging, visuals, and tone align across all platforms. A strong brand creates recognition and loyalty.

As your business grows, consider creating strategic partnerships. Collaborating with other businesses can expand your reach and provide additional value to your customers. Look for complementary brands that share your values. This could mean co-hosting events, joint marketing campaigns, or cross-promoting products. Leverage each other's audiences to drive growth.

Let's not forget about technology. In today's world, leveraging technology is not optional; it's a necessity. Invest in tools that can automate tasks, analyze data, and streamline your operations. This could be anything from CRM systems to project management software. The right tech stack can enhance efficiency, reduce costs, and improve customer experiences.

Speaking of customer experiences, prioritize them. A seamless, enjoyable experience can set you apart from the competition. From the moment a customer interacts with your brand, they should feel valued. This includes everything from your website's user experience to customer service interactions.

Implement a customer relationship management (CRM) system to track interactions and personalize communication. When customers feel valued and understood, they're more likely to become repeat buyers. Remember, it's cheaper to retain a customer than to acquire a new one.

Now, let's talk about adaptability. The market is always shifting, and your business needs to be agile. Monitor industry trends, economic shifts, and consumer behaviors. Be prepared to pivot when necessary. This doesn't mean you should jump on every trend; rather, assess what aligns with your business model and customer needs.

Consider running experiments. Try out new ideas on a small scale before fully committing. This allows you to test the waters without risking too much. Collect data, analyze results, and make informed decisions based on what works. Experimentation is a powerful tool for innovation.

As you build your business, don't forget about your team. Your employees are the backbone of your operation. Invest in their growth and development. Create a positive company culture that fosters collaboration, innovation, and accountability. When your team feels valued, they're more likely to go above and beyond for your business.

Regularly check in with your team to gauge morale and address any concerns. Foster open communication and encourage feedback. When everyone is on the same page, you create a stronger, more resilient organization.

Let's talk about financial health. You need to keep a close eye on your cash flow. Create a budget and stick to it. Monitor your income and expenses regularly. If you're not financially literate, invest time in learning the basics. Understand your profit margins, break-even point, and overall financial picture. This knowledge is critical for making informed decisions.

As your business grows, consider bringing in a financial advisor. They can provide valuable insights and help you navigate complex financial decisions. Having someone with expertise can give you peace of mind and ensure you're on the right track.

Now, let's touch on the importance of sustainability—not just environmentally, but in terms of business practices. Customers today are increasingly conscious of the impact of their purchases. Consider how your business can contribute to sustainability. This could be through eco-friendly practices, sourcing materials responsibly, or giving back to the community.

When you align your business with values that resonate with your customers, you build loyalty and attract like-minded individuals. People want to support brands that share their values.

Finally, let's talk about long-term vision. What do you want your business to achieve in the next 5, 10, or even 20 years? Set clear goals and create a roadmap to get there. This isn't just about revenue; consider the impact you want to make and the legacy you want to leave behind.

Regularly review and adjust your goals as needed. Stay adaptable but focused. A clear vision keeps you motivated and aligned with your purpose. This is about building something that transcends your own personal wealth.

In conclusion, crafting a sustainable business model is about understanding your value proposition, knowing your market, diversifying your income streams, and building resilience. It's about creating a brand that resonates, leveraging technology, and prioritizing customer experiences.

Stay agile, invest in your team, and keep your financial health in check. Embrace sustainability and maintain a long-term vision. When you build a resilient business, you're setting yourself up for long-term success—so rich that you'll start questioning the meaning of money. Let's get to work and build something extraordinary!

4.1 Mastering Sales and Marketing

Alright, let's dive into the nitty-gritty of sales and marketing. If you want to build wealth that makes you question the very meaning of money, you've got to master these two elements. This isn't just fluff; it's the backbone of any successful business. You can have the best product in the world, but if nobody knows about it, or if you can't close the deal, you're dead in the water.

First, let's talk about sales. Sales isn't a dirty word. It's not some sleazy hustle; it's about serving people. When you shift your mindset from "I'm selling" to "I'm helping," everything changes. You're not pushing a product; you're providing a solution to someone's problem. You need to understand your audience's pain points deeply. What keeps them up at night? What are their biggest challenges? Once you figure that out, your job becomes much easier.

Here's the thing: sales is all about relationships. People buy from those they trust. Building rapport is critical. You want to create a connection with your prospects. Listen more than you talk. Ask questions, dig deep, and genuinely understand their needs. The more you know about them, the better you can position your offering as the solution they've been looking for.

Now, let's discuss the art of storytelling. You want to craft a narrative around your product. This isn't just about features and benefits; it's about painting a picture of how your product changes lives. Share success stories, testimonials, and case studies. People remember stories. Make your customer the hero and position your product as the tool that helps them win.

But don't just rely on your own stories. Encourage your customers to share theirs too. User-generated content can be a powerful marketing tool. When potential customers see real people having real success with your product, it builds trust. It's social proof, and it's incredibly persuasive.

Now, let's pivot to closing the sale. This is where the rubber meets the road. You need to be confident. If you're hesitant or uncertain, your prospects will pick up on that. Practice your pitch until it feels second nature. You should be able to articulate the value of your product clearly and concisely.

Use urgency and scarcity effectively. If people think they can come back later, they often will. Create a sense of urgency around your offers. This could be a limited-time discount, a bonus for signing up today, or highlighting limited availability. But be ethical about it. Don't fabricate scarcity; it has to be real.

Let's discuss follow-up. This is a game-changer. Many sales are lost simply because people don't follow up. If someone shows interest but doesn't buy right away, don't just let it go. Follow up with them. Send an email, make a phone call, or reach out on social media. Keep the conversation going.

Timing is crucial here. People are busy, and they often need multiple touchpoints before making a decision. Be persistent, but don't be pushy. Remember, you're building a relationship, not just closing a sale.

Now, let's talk marketing. This is where you create awareness around your product or service. You've got to get in front of the right people. Start with defining your target audience. Who are they? What do they care about? What channels do they use? This will guide all your marketing efforts.

Content marketing is an excellent way to establish authority in your niche. Create valuable content that educates and informs your audience. Blog posts, videos, podcasts—whatever medium resonates with your target market. When you provide value upfront, people will see you as an expert. This builds trust and makes them more likely to consider your product when they're ready to buy.

Social media is a powerful tool for marketing, but you've got to be strategic. Don't just post for the sake of posting. Have a plan. Determine what types of content you'll share and when. Engage with your audience. Respond to comments, answer questions, and be active in conversations. This isn't just about broadcasting your message; it's about creating a community.

Email marketing is still one of the highest ROI strategies out there. Build an email list and nurture those leads. Share valuable content, promote your offers, and keep your audience engaged. Personalization is key here. Use their names, segment your list, and tailor your messages based on their interests. When people feel like you're speaking directly to them, they're much more likely to take action.

Now, let's talk about paid advertising. This can be a fantastic way to scale your efforts, but you need to approach it wisely. Start by setting a budget. Determine how much you're willing to spend and stick to it. Research your target audience and craft compelling ad copy that resonates with them. Test different creatives and messaging to see what performs best. This is an iterative process, so don't be afraid to experiment and optimize.

Analytics are your best friend. You need to track what's working and what's not. Use tools like Google Analytics, social media insights, and email performance metrics to gather data. This will help you refine your strategies over time. If something isn't performing, don't be afraid to pivot. You want to invest your time and money in what drives results.

Don't forget about SEO. Search engine optimization is essential for getting organic traffic to your website. Optimize your content for relevant keywords, and ensure your site is user-friendly. The higher you rank on search engines, the more visibility you gain. This is a long-term strategy, but it pays off big time in the end.

Another powerful marketing strategy is networking. Building relationships with other entrepreneurs, influencers, or industry leaders can open up new opportunities. Attend events, join relevant groups, and participate in discussions. Don't be afraid to reach out to others. Offer value first—whether it's sharing insights, collaborating on projects, or promoting their work. When you build genuine relationships, you create a network that can help elevate your business.

Now, let's shift gears and discuss the importance of branding. Your brand is more than just a logo; it's your identity. It's how your audience perceives you. Invest time in defining your brand's voice, mission, and values. Ensure that everything—from your website to your social media profiles—reflects your brand consistently. A strong brand fosters trust and recognition.

Let's talk about pricing. This is often a tricky subject, but it's crucial. Your pricing should reflect the value you provide. Don't undervalue yourself. Research your competitors and understand what the market is willing to pay. Pricing isn't just about covering costs; it's about positioning your brand. Higher prices can imply higher quality, but make sure you deliver on that promise.

Consider offering tiered pricing. This allows you to cater to different segments of your audience. Have a basic package for budget-conscious customers and premium options for those willing to invest more. This not only broadens your reach but also increases your average transaction value.

As you grow, think about expanding your product line. Upselling and cross-selling can significantly boost your revenue. If someone buys a product, offer complementary items. If they're interested in your basic service, promote your premium package. This adds value to your customers and increases your bottom line.

Let's wrap up by talking about mindset. Mastering sales and marketing requires a growth mindset. You will face challenges and setbacks, but don't let them deter you. Learn from every experience, whether it's a successful sale or a lost opportunity. Stay curious, keep testing new strategies, and never stop learning.

Surround yourself with people who inspire you and challenge you to grow. Join communities, attend workshops, or find mentors who can provide guidance. The more you invest in your personal development, the more equipped you'll be to master sales and marketing.

Ultimately, mastering sales and marketing is about understanding your audience, building relationships, and providing value. It's about telling compelling stories and creating experiences that resonate. When you get this right, you'll create a sales machine that drives your business forward.

You want to be so good at sales and marketing that you can generate revenue effortlessly. This is what separates the mediocre from the extraordinary. So dive in, get your hands dirty, and start mastering the skills that will propel you to wealth. You've got this!

4.2 Developing a High-Performing Team

Let's get into it. If you want to create wealth that makes you question the meaning of money, you can't do it alone. You need a high-performing team behind you. This isn't just about hiring warm bodies; it's about assembling a group of driven individuals who are aligned with your vision and goals. When you nail this, you set the stage for incredible success.

First off, it all starts with clarity. You need to be crystal clear on your vision. What are you trying to achieve? Where are you headed? If you can't articulate this to your team, you're setting them up for failure. People need a north star to guide them. Share your vision often and in various ways—meetings, emails, team huddles. Make it a part of your culture.

Now, let's talk about hiring. This is critical. You want to look beyond resumes. Skills are important, but attitude is everything. You can train someone on specific tasks, but you can't change their mindset. Look for people who are hungry, adaptable, and ready to roll up their sleeves. During interviews, ask questions that reveal their character. "Tell me about a time you faced a challenge. How did you handle it?" The answers will give you insight into how they think and how they'll fit into your culture.

Once you have your team in place, it's time to empower them. Micromanaging is a killer. Trust your people to do their jobs. Give them the autonomy to make decisions. When you empower your team, you create ownership. They feel responsible for their work, and that leads to higher quality and better results. Set clear expectations and then let them figure out how to meet those expectations.

Communication is vital here. You want to foster an environment where everyone feels comfortable sharing ideas and feedback. Create regular check-ins, whether they're one-on-ones or team meetings. Encourage open dialogue. Let your team know that their voices matter. When people feel heard, they're more engaged and motivated.

Now, let's talk about collaboration. Encourage teamwork. Create opportunities for your team to work together on projects. This not only strengthens relationships but also sparks creativity. When diverse minds come together, magic happens. Ideas flow, problems get solved, and innovation takes off. Foster an atmosphere where collaboration is not just encouraged but expected.

Recognize and celebrate achievements, big and small. When someone hits a milestone or goes above and beyond, shout it from the rooftops! This could be through public recognition, rewards, or simple shout-outs in meetings. Celebrating successes boosts morale and reinforces a culture of excellence. People want to be part of a winning team, so make sure they know when they're winning.

Feedback is another crucial component. Regularly provide constructive feedback to your team. Don't wait until annual reviews to have these conversations. Feedback should be ongoing. If someone's doing something well, let them know. If there's an area for improvement, address it promptly. This helps your team grow and develop continuously. Create a feedback loop where they can also provide input on your leadership. This builds trust and respect.

Invest in their development. Provide opportunities for your team to learn new skills. Whether it's workshops, courses, or mentorship programs, support their growth. When you invest in their future, they'll invest in yours. This isn't just a perk; it's an expectation. People want to know that they're growing in their careers. When they see you're committed to their development, they'll be more engaged and loyal.

Let's talk about diversity. A diverse team brings different perspectives, which leads to better decision-making and creativity. Don't just check the box on diversity; make it a core part of your hiring process. Look for candidates from various backgrounds, experiences, and cultures. This diversity will enrich your team and improve your outcomes.

Now, you can't ignore the importance of culture. Your team's culture will dictate how they operate, so be intentional about it. What do you want your culture to look like? Write it down, and live it. Set the tone from the top. If you value transparency, be transparent. If you prioritize innovation, encourage experimentation. Your culture is the environment in which your team will thrive or wither.

Establish core values that reflect your mission. These values should guide every decision and behavior within your organization. Make sure everyone on your team understands and embodies these values. When your team is aligned with your values, they're more likely to work harmoniously toward your common goals.

Let's dive into accountability. You can't have a high-performing team without accountability. Set clear metrics and KPIs for every role. Make sure everyone knows what's expected of them and how their performance will be measured. Hold regular performance reviews, but don't just focus on the numbers. Discuss growth, areas for improvement, and future goals. This accountability drives performance and ensures everyone is pulling in the same direction.

When challenges arise, and they will, you need to lead by example. Be the calm in the storm. Your team will look to you for guidance. If you freak out, they'll freak out. Stay composed, focus on solutions, and encourage your team to do the same. This builds resilience within your team. When they see you handle adversity with grace, they'll be more likely to emulate that behavior.

Now, let's talk about motivation. People are motivated by different things. Some crave recognition, while others are driven by the mission or the impact of their work. Get to know your team members as individuals. Find out what motivates each of them and leverage that to keep them engaged. Tailor your approach to their specific needs.

Encourage innovation within your team. Create a safe space for them to share new ideas without fear of judgment. Regularly hold brainstorming sessions where everyone can contribute. Some of the best ideas come from the least expected places. If someone has a crazy idea, don't shut it down immediately. Explore it. It might lead to a breakthrough.

Remember to balance workloads. Burnout is real, and it can derail even the best teams. Monitor your team's stress levels and workload. Make adjustments as needed. If someone is overwhelmed, redistribute tasks or offer support. A well-rested, balanced team performs better than one that's burned out.

As your business grows, you'll need to scale your team. This means developing leaders within your organization. Identify high-potential individuals and invest in their growth. Provide leadership training, mentorship, and opportunities to take on more responsibility. When you create leaders, you multiply your effectiveness. This will ensure that your organization can handle growth and adapt to challenges.

Let's wrap this up with a focus on results. High-performing teams are results-oriented. Celebrate outcomes, not just efforts. It's great to work hard, but at the end of the day, you need results. Align your team around common goals and hold each other accountable for achieving them.

Regularly assess your team's performance. Analyze what's working and what's not. Use metrics to gauge success, but also rely on qualitative feedback. Listen to your team and adjust strategies as needed. Stay agile and willing to pivot when circumstances change.

In conclusion, developing a high-performing team isn't just a nice-to-have; it's essential for building wealth and achieving your vision. Be clear about your goals, hire for attitude, empower your people, and foster collaboration. Celebrate successes, provide ongoing feedback, and invest in your team's growth.

Create a culture that values diversity, accountability, and innovation. Lead by example during tough times, and prioritize motivation and well-being. Build leaders within your organization, and focus relentlessly on results.

When you master the art of building a high-performing team, you'll create a powerhouse capable of achieving extraordinary things. You'll be so successful that the meaning of money will become a secondary consideration in your journey. Now go out there and build that team!

Chapter 5

Financial Mastery and Wealth Preservation

Understanding Financial Literacy

Let's cut to the chase: if you want to be so wealthy you start questioning the very meaning of money, you need to get your financial literacy dialed in. This isn't just about making money; it's about mastering how to keep it and grow it. Financial literacy isn't optional—it's essential. You wouldn't drive a car without knowing how it works, right? So why would you handle your finances without understanding the basics?

First off, let's talk about cash flow. This is the lifeblood of any business or individual. You've got to know where your money is coming from and where it's going. It's not enough to just earn money; you need to track it meticulously. Create a simple cash flow statement. It'll help you visualize your income and expenses. Trust me, you want to know this stuff.

Now, let's break down income. There are two types: active and passive. Active income is what you earn from your job or business—this is trading your time for money. Passive income, on the other hand, is money that comes in without you having to actively work for it. Think investments, rental income, royalties. You want to build up that passive income stream. The more passive income you have, the less you have to worry about your day-to-day financial situation.

So, how do you create those passive streams? Start by investing. I'm not talking about throwing money into stocks and hoping for the best. You need to understand the market. Learn about different asset classes—real estate, stocks, bonds, and more. Diversification is key here. Don't put all your eggs in one basket.

Real estate can be a gold mine. Whether it's rental properties or flipping houses, it's a fantastic way to build wealth. Understand the numbers: cash flow, appreciation, and ROI. A well-chosen property can provide consistent cash flow and appreciate over time. That's a win-win.

Next, let's talk about stocks. They can be volatile, but with proper knowledge and strategy, they can grow your wealth significantly. Understand the companies you're investing in. Do your due diligence. Read financial statements, listen to earnings calls, and analyze market trends. You want to be informed, not just following the latest trend or hot tip.

Bonds are another option. They're generally less risky than stocks and can provide steady income. They won't make you rich overnight, but they add stability to your portfolio. Think of them as the calm waters in your financial ocean.

Now, let's pivot to expenses. You have to control your spending. It's easy to let lifestyle creep sneak in. One minute you're living within your means, and the next, you're maxing out your credit cards because you "deserve it." No. You don't deserve to be broke. Track your expenses religiously. Use apps or spreadsheets to categorize and analyze where your money goes.

Create a budget that aligns with your financial goals. Cut unnecessary expenses ruthlessly. You don't need the latest gadget if you can't afford it. Prioritize your spending. Ask yourself, "Is this a want or a need?" If it's a want, evaluate how it fits into your long-term financial picture.

Let's dive into debt management. Not all debt is created equal. Some debt can be a tool to help you build wealth—like a mortgage on an investment property. But consumer debt? That's a trap. High-interest debt will suck your financial health dry. Focus on paying off that debt as quickly as possible. Start with the highest interest rates first—this is called the avalanche method.

Once you've tackled the high-interest debt, consider the snowball method. Pay off the smallest debts first to build momentum. This can be motivating. As you clear those debts, you'll feel a psychological lift that propels you to tackle larger amounts.

Next, let's discuss savings. You need to have an emergency fund. Aim for three to six months' worth of living expenses. This provides a safety net when life throws curveballs at you. When you're financially secure, you can take calculated risks in other areas.

Invest your savings wisely. Don't just let it sit in a savings account earning paltry interest. Look for high-yield savings accounts or consider certificates of deposit (CDs) for short-term savings goals. If you're looking at the long term, contribute to retirement accounts like a 401(k) or an IRA. Take advantage of employer matches—it's free money!

Insurance is another critical component of financial literacy. You need to protect your assets. Health insurance, life insurance, disability insurance—these are must-haves. You don't want to go bankrupt from a medical emergency. Review your coverage regularly to ensure it aligns with your needs.

Now, let's talk about taxes. Understanding the tax code can save you a fortune. Don't just shove your paperwork to an accountant and hope for the best. Get educated on tax strategies. Look into deductions, credits, and different structures for your business. An S-Corp, LLC, or C-Corp can have different tax implications.

Learn about capital gains tax. If you sell an asset for more than you bought it, that profit is taxed. Long-term capital gains are taxed at a lower rate than short-term, so hold onto your investments if you can. Use tax-advantaged accounts to minimize your tax burden.

Financial literacy also means knowing when to seek help. Sometimes, you need to bring in an expert—financial advisors, accountants, or tax professionals. Don't be afraid to invest in their services if it'll lead to better decision-making. Just make sure to do your homework. Find professionals who align with your goals and values.

Let's not forget about the power of networking. Surround yourself with financially literate people. Join groups or communities focused on personal finance and investing. Share experiences, ask questions, and learn from each other. The right network can provide insights you might never find on your own.

Now, let's pivot to mindset. Your relationship with money plays a massive role in your financial success. You've got to view money as a tool—not a goal. It's a means to create the life you want, to help others, and to build a legacy. When you shift your mindset from scarcity to abundance, you start making better financial decisions.

You also need to embrace lifelong learning. The financial landscape is always changing. Stay informed about market trends, economic shifts, and new investment opportunities. Read books, listen to podcasts, take courses.

The more knowledgeable you become, the more confident you'll be in making financial decisions.

Let's talk about setting financial goals. You need clear, measurable objectives. Whether it's saving for a home, funding your kids' education, or building a retirement nest egg, define your goals. Break them down into actionable steps. This makes them less daunting and gives you a roadmap to follow.

Review your goals regularly. Are you on track? Do you need to make adjustments? Life changes, and so should your financial plan. Stay flexible and adapt to new circumstances.

Another critical element is understanding risk. All investments carry risk, but that doesn't mean you should avoid it altogether. Assess your risk tolerance. Are you comfortable with high-risk, high-reward investments, or do you prefer steady, low-risk options? Knowing your risk tolerance will guide your investment decisions.

Also, don't be afraid of failure. Everyone experiences setbacks. It's part of the journey. What matters is how you respond. Learn from your mistakes, adjust your strategy, and keep pushing forward. Failure is often the best teacher.

Lastly, think long-term. Wealth isn't built overnight. It takes time, patience, and consistency. Focus on sustainable growth rather than quick wins. Stay disciplined with your savings and investments. Trust the process, and remember that the journey to financial mastery is a marathon, not a sprint.

In summary, understanding financial literacy is the foundation for building wealth. Master cash flow, income diversification, and expenses. Control your debt and prioritize savings. Protect your assets with insurance, and be savvy about taxes. Seek help when needed, network with financially savvy individuals, and embrace a mindset of abundance.

Set clear financial goals and remain flexible. Understand your risk tolerance and learn from your mistakes. Stay committed to lifelong learning and remember that building wealth is a long-term endeavor.

When you master these principles, you'll be on the path to creating wealth so significant that you'll start questioning the meaning of money itself. Now go out there and make it happen!

5.1 Smart Investing Strategies

Let's dive into the nitty-gritty of investing. If you want to accumulate wealth that makes you question the very meaning of money, you've got to get smart about where you put your cash. This isn't a game; it's your future we're talking about. So, let's break down some strategies that can take you from a novice to a savvy investor.

First things first: know your investment goals. Are you looking for short-term gains or long-term wealth accumulation? Clarity here is crucial. If you don't know what you want, how can you make a plan? Define your objectives. Maybe you want to retire early, fund your kid's education, or simply build a safety net. Whatever it is, write it down. Make it real.

Once you've got your goals lined up, it's time to build a diversified portfolio. This is your safety net. Diversification means spreading your investments across various asset classes—stocks, bonds, real estate, commodities, and maybe some alternative investments. Think of it like this: don't put all your eggs in one basket. If one basket falls, you want to make sure you've got others to catch your eggs.

Let's talk about stocks. They can be a great way to grow wealth over time, but they're also volatile. Understand the different types of stocks: growth stocks, value stocks, and dividend-paying stocks. Growth stocks are companies that are expected to grow at an above-average rate. These can be risky but can yield high returns. Value stocks, on the other hand, are undervalued companies that have strong fundamentals. They're the hidden gems you want to find.

Then you have dividend stocks. These pay you to own them, often providing a steady income stream while you wait for the stock to appreciate. Reinvest those dividends to compound your returns over time. This is the magic of compound interest—earning interest on your interest.

Next, let's hit bonds. They're generally safer than stocks and provide a steady income. Think of them as the calm in your financial storm. When the stock market gets shaky, bonds can stabilize your portfolio. Understand the different types of bonds: government bonds, municipal bonds, and corporate bonds. Each has its own risk and return profile.

Real estate is another powerful investment vehicle. It's not just about flipping houses or being a landlord; it's about building assets that appreciate over time. Rental properties can provide cash flow while also increasing in value. Do your homework. Analyze market trends, understand neighborhood dynamics, and always calculate potential returns before diving in.

Let's not overlook index funds and ETFs (exchange-traded funds). These are perfect for those who want to invest without the headache of picking individual stocks. They offer built-in diversification because they track entire indexes like the S&P 500. They're low-cost, which means more of your money goes toward your investments and not fees.

Now, while we're talking about costs, let's address fees. Understand what you're paying for. High fees can eat away at your returns over time. Look for low-cost options and always ask about hidden fees. Transparency is key. You want to know where your money is going.

Let's get a little deeper into the concept of dollar-cost averaging. This strategy involves consistently investing a fixed amount of money at regular intervals, regardless of the market conditions. This takes the emotion out of investing. Instead of trying to time the market—good luck with that—you're buying in all the time. Over time, this can lower your average cost per share. It's a powerful way to build wealth without getting caught up in the daily noise of the market.

Speaking of noise, let's talk about mindset. When you're investing, it's easy to get caught up in the hype—everyone's talking about the next big stock, and you feel the pressure to jump in. Don't. Stick to your strategy. Be patient. Investing is a marathon, not a sprint. The market goes up and down; that's just part of the game. Your goal is to stay the course and focus on long-term growth.

Set up an investment policy statement (IPS) for yourself. This is your game plan. It outlines your investment goals, strategies, risk tolerance, and how you'll make adjustments. When the market gets rocky, your IPS keeps you grounded. It's a reminder of why you're investing and how you plan to do it.

As you grow your portfolio, consider tax implications. Capital gains tax can take a bite out of your profits, so understand how to minimize your tax liability. Utilize tax-advantaged accounts like IRAs and 401(k)s. These accounts can help you defer taxes or even avoid them altogether. It's all about keeping more of what you earn.

Let's touch on real estate investment trusts (REITs). These are a fantastic way to invest in real estate without having to buy physical properties. REITs pool money from multiple investors to purchase, operate, or finance income-generating real estate. They offer dividends and the potential for capital appreciation, making them an attractive option for many investors.

Now, let's get tactical. When evaluating a potential investment, ask yourself three questions: Is it scalable? Does it have a competitive advantage? What are the risks involved? If the answer to these questions is favorable, you might have a winner on your hands.

Keep an eye on emerging markets. These can be risky but offer potential for significant returns. As economies develop, companies in those regions can experience explosive growth. Just remember to do your homework. Understand the political and economic environment before diving in.

You also want to consider alternative investments. Think of assets like art, collectibles, or even cryptocurrencies. These can diversify your portfolio and provide potential returns that are uncorrelated with traditional markets. But tread carefully—these markets can be speculative, and you should only allocate a small portion of your portfolio to them.

Let's talk about real estate again, specifically house hacking. This is a strategy where you buy a multi-family property, live in one unit, and rent out the others. This can significantly reduce your living expenses while also building equity. It's a smart way to get into real estate without a massive upfront investment.

Another approach is to leverage your home. If you have equity in your primary residence, consider a home equity line of credit (HELOC). This can provide you with funds to invest in other opportunities while keeping your cash flow intact. Just be cautious; this isn't free money. You're putting your home on the line, so ensure you have a solid plan for repayment.

As you refine your investing strategies, always stay informed. The financial landscape is constantly changing. Keep an eye on market trends, economic indicators, and news that could impact your investments. Knowledge is power. The more informed you are, the better decisions you can make.

Consider joining investment clubs or communities. Surround yourself with like-minded individuals who share your goals. You can learn a ton from others' experiences, successes, and failures. Networking can also open doors to investment opportunities you might not find on your own.

Let's not forget about the power of mentorship. Find someone who's been in the game longer than you. A mentor can provide invaluable insights, guidance, and a fresh perspective. Learn from their mistakes and successes to fast-track your own journey.

Finally, develop a exit strategy for each investment. Know when to sell or pivot. This isn't just about buying and holding; sometimes, you need to cut your losses. Having a plan for how and when to exit an investment is critical for preserving your wealth.

In conclusion, smart investing isn't just about picking the right stocks or timing the market. It's about having a strategy, staying disciplined, and being informed. Define your goals, diversify your portfolio, and always look for opportunities to grow your wealth.

Investing is a powerful tool for building wealth, and when done right, it can lead to financial freedom and the kind of wealth that makes you question the meaning of money itself. Now get out there and start investing smarter!

5.2 Protecting Your Wealth

Let's face it: building wealth is just half the battle. The other half? keeping everything you've earned safe. All of your hard work might be in vain if you don't have a sound plan in place to preserve your riches. We're discussing protecting your assets from litigation, market declines, and even unforeseen life circumstances. So let's get started and learn how to safeguard your hard-earned money.

Let's start by discussing insurance, which is the most fundamental form of protection. Though it's important, this isn't the most glamorous subject. I take it that you wouldn't use a vehicle without insurance? So why would you take a different strategy to your possessions or your life? Having liability, house, vehicle, and health insurance is essential. Regularly review your policies. Don't simply sign and go on. Make sure you have adequate insurance to safeguard both your riches and your way of life.

Let's go more specific now. Now let's discuss umbrella insurance. On steroids, this is your safety net. Umbrella insurance kicks in if you are sued for more than your standard liability coverage. It's like to having a superhero guard your possessions. You may insure against millions of liabilities for a few hundred dollars annually. If you have assets to safeguard, it should go without saying.

Next, think about ways to secure your assets. These are sophisticated strategies that can protect your cash against litigation and creditors. Consider establishing a trust or an LLC. Your corporate responsibilities and personal assets can be kept apart with the use of an LLC. This implies that your personal assets, such as your house and money, are usually safeguarded in the event that your company is sued.

Trusts can offer an additional degree of protection. They can shield your assets from litigation, creditors, and even the probate process. A trust may guarantee that your assets are dispersed in accordance with your intentions without undergoing the drawn-out probate procedure, which is beneficial if you're concerned about what will happen to your riches after you die away.

Then there is the value of diversity, which applies to both your asset ownership and your investments. Avoid taking on too much at once. Distribute your capital throughout many asset types. equities, bonds, real estate, and even unconventional assets. You don't want your whole financial situation to collapse if one industry collapses.

Let's now discuss keeping an emergency fund up to date. This serves as your safety net. Three to six months' worth of living expenditures should be your goal. This is for life's tiny shocks, such as an unforeseen auto repair or medical cost, not simply for sudden job loss. When life throws you a curveball, you don't have to take money out of your investments or incur debt since you have this fund.

Next, think about tax tactics. A sound tax strategy may save your money from needless depletion. Speak with a tax expert who is aware of your financial circumstances. They can assist you in identifying credits, deductions, and strategies to reduce your tax obligation. This is about managing your finances wisely, not about avoiding taxes. Don't give Uncle Sam more than is required because you've worked hard for every dime.

Let's change the subject and discuss estate planning. Although it's not the most interesting subject, you should think about what will happen to your fortune once you pass away. Make a will. This is your asset distribution road map. You don't want the state to make decisions for you if you don't have one.

When making healthcare decisions, think about using an advanced directive or living will. Ensure that your loved ones are aware of your desires. In addition to safeguarding your possessions, this also provides you comfort in knowing that your family won't be left behind at a trying time.

Think about getting life insurance if you have dependents. In the event that you pass away, this guarantees your loved ones' financial stability. Select a policy that will pay for your family's necessities as well as your bills and mortgage. The future of your family may be safeguarded by this safety net.

Let's now discuss keeping an eye on your riches. What you don't track, you can't defend. Pay attention to your credit reports, investments, and bank accounts. Financial ruin can result from identity theft, which is genuine. Examine your credit report on a regular basis and think about signing up for a credit monitoring program. Do anything right away if something seems strange.

Another topic to concentrate on is cybersecurity. The hazards to your money increase along with it. Make sure your financial accounts have strong, one-of-a-kind passwords. Whenever feasible, turn on two-factor authentication. Your financial information should not be left out in the open like a banquet for criminals. As much as your money depends on it, so does your data.

Not to be overlooked is the significance of a financial advisor. A competent adviser can offer customized plans to safeguard and increase your money. They can keep you on course and guide you through tricky financial situations. Select a person who has a fiduciary obligation to look out for your best interests. Creating a thorough financial strategy that takes risk management, estate planning, and investing techniques into account is more important than simply choosing stocks.

Understanding market risks is another essential component of wealth preservation. The market is erratic. When things go wrong, have a plan. Recognize your level of risk tolerance and modify your portfolio appropriately. Think about making a more cautious allocation if you can't bear the thought of a market meltdown. Getting a good night's sleep is more important than pursuing riskier profits.

Let's now discuss liability threats in more detail. Being a business owner exposes you to greater danger than the typical person. If you offer services, think about getting professional liability insurance. This can shield you from legal action resulting from your company's activities. Keep business and personal assets separate; don't let one influence the other.

The emotional component of riches cannot be disregarded. We frequently associate money with who we are. Be mindful of the impact wealth has on your relationships as you accumulate it. Family and friends may become tense, envious, or have irrational expectations due to wealth. Establish limits. Openly discuss your financial status with individuals who are important to you. This can lessen miscommunications and possible disputes.

Maintain flexibility in your financial strategies. Your tactics should evolve as life does. Review your protection plans and financial objectives on a regular basis. This year, what worked last year might not work. As necessary, make modifications.

And never forget that saying no is OK. As your fortune increases, friends, family, and even complete strangers will approach you with "can't-miss" investment possibilities. Have discernment. Be careful where you spend your money to safeguard your fortune. You shouldn't accept a "great deal" just because someone offers it to you.

Let's talk about the value of knowledge as well. You can safeguard your cash more effectively if you have greater knowledge. Keep up with changes in the market, new investment vehicles, and financial trends. Invest in your financial education by reading books, listening to podcasts, and going to seminars.

Be in the company of a strong network of mentors, advisers, and people who share your values. Their knowledge might be very helpful. In addition to offering assistance, a strong network keeps you up to date on any dangers and possibilities.

Staying ahead of scammers is another way to safeguard your cash. Criminals are constantly searching for methods to take advantage of the gullible. Learn about typical scams and warning signs. Generally speaking, if something seems too good to be true, it is. Have faith in your gut and conduct thorough research.

Finally, develop an abundant attitude while maintaining a realistic perspective. Wealth is not a destination; it is a tool. It is intended to provide you possibilities, support you and your loved ones, and empower you. However, it also entails obligations. Keep everything you've created safe so you may enjoy it to the fullest without worrying about losing it.

In conclusion, safeguarding your wealth is equally as crucial as creating it. Use tax preparation, asset protection techniques, and insurance to bolster your defenses. Make a thorough estate plan, keep an eye on your fortune, and be aware of market dangers. Keep yourself informed about financial concerns and surround yourself with reliable experts.

This is how you leave a lasting legacy in addition to protecting your possessions. You're building a life that represents your beliefs, objectives, and goals rather than merely amassing cash. Now go out there and defend what you've put so much effort into creating!

Chapter 6
The Purpose Beyond Profit

Philanthropy and Social Impact

We're going to dive into something crucial today—something that transcends the numbers, the hustle, and the grind. It's about purpose. You see, money is powerful, but what you do with that power? That's where the real magic happens. Let's talk about philanthropy and social impact, and why they should matter to you, not just as a wealthy individual, but as a human being navigating this world.

First, let's clear the air. Philanthropy isn't just for the billionaires or those who've hit it big overnight. It's for everyone. If you have the ability to make an impact, you have a responsibility to do so. This doesn't mean you have to write million-dollar checks right away. It means being intentional about the resources—time, money, skills—you have. It's about understanding that wealth can be a tool for change.

We live in a society where the wealth gap is widening. The middle class is shrinking, and the issues are becoming more visible. Climate change, education disparities, healthcare access—these are not just buzzwords; they're real challenges we all face. So, if you're in a position to help, why wouldn't you? Your contribution can be the catalyst for real change.

Think of it this way: you've worked hard to build your wealth, but what happens when you're gone? Do you want your legacy to be just another bank account balance? Or do you want to leave behind something meaningful? Philanthropy allows you to shape your legacy. It's about creating a narrative around your wealth—a story that goes beyond the numbers and reflects your values.

Now, let's unpack what philanthropy really means. It's not just about giving money; it's about making a meaningful impact. You want to be strategic about where your resources go. Don't just throw money at every cause that sounds good. Take a step back and evaluate what resonates with you. What issues ignite your passion?

For instance, if you care deeply about education, consider funding scholarships, supporting after-school programs, or even starting your own educational initiative. If healthcare is your focus, maybe you can contribute to clinics in underserved communities. The key is alignment. Your contributions should reflect your values and beliefs.

Let's talk about social impact investing. This is where you can put your money to work while also making a difference. You don't have to choose between profit and purpose. Social impact investing seeks to generate positive social or environmental impact alongside financial returns. Think of it as a way to be a conscious capitalist.

Venture philanthropy is another approach. It combines the principles of venture capital with philanthropy. This means you're not just giving money; you're investing in organizations or initiatives that have the potential for growth and scalability. You want to empower those who are already making a difference but may need the capital to expand their reach.

One of the best parts of philanthropy is the opportunity to collaborate. You don't have to do this alone. Partnering with like-minded individuals or organizations can amplify your impact. Pool resources, share knowledge, and create a coalition for change. Together, you can tackle challenges that one person or organization might struggle with alone.

But here's a word of caution: avoid being a "check writer" without involvement. Philanthropy should be hands-on. When you engage with the communities you're trying to help, you gain valuable insights that money alone can't provide. Listen to the needs of those you're serving. Understand their challenges, and tailor your approach accordingly. This not only increases the effectiveness of your contributions but also fosters trust and respect.

Let's talk about the psychology of giving. It's powerful. Research shows that acts of kindness and generosity boost our well-being. When you give, it creates a sense of purpose and fulfillment. You feel connected to something larger than yourself. It's a win-win situation—your wealth does good, and you experience a boost in happiness.

Incorporating philanthropy into your life doesn't have to be daunting. Start small. Volunteer your time at a local charity or mentor someone in your field. These small acts create ripples that can lead to significant change. As you grow, consider setting up a charitable foundation. This not only allows you to manage your giving but also provides tax benefits. It's a smart financial move while making a difference.

When thinking about philanthropy, embrace the concept of "impact measurement." Just like you would track your business performance, measure the effectiveness of your philanthropic efforts. What outcomes are you achieving? Are you making a tangible difference? Use data to guide your decisions and refine your approach. This ensures that your contributions are as effective as possible.

Let's not forget the importance of storytelling. People connect with stories. When you share the impact of your contributions—whether through social media, blog posts, or community events—you inspire others to join the cause. Highlight success stories, showcase the change you're helping to create. This not only raises awareness but also builds a community of supporters around your mission.

Your network can be a powerful ally in your philanthropic journey. Leverage your connections to raise awareness and resources for your chosen causes. Host events, panel discussions, or fundraisers that bring people together for a common purpose. Engaging your network not only amplifies your impact but also fosters a sense of community.

As you step into the realm of philanthropy, be prepared for challenges. Not every initiative will be a slam dunk. There will be setbacks, failures, and moments of frustration. But that's part of the process. Embrace it. Learn from your mistakes and adapt your strategies. Resilience is key. Your willingness to learn and pivot will ultimately lead to greater impact.

When you get involved in philanthropy, you also have a unique opportunity to inspire the next generation. Share your experiences with your children, nieces, or nephews. Teach them the importance of giving back. Help them understand that wealth isn't just about accumulation; it's about contribution. Show them that making a difference is not only rewarding but also essential for building a better world.

Consider creating a family philanthropy program. This can be a powerful way to involve your family in giving back. Set aside a portion of your wealth to support causes as a family. Discuss together what matters most to each family member, and make decisions collaboratively. This not only strengthens family bonds but also instills values of generosity and social responsibility.

Let's get tactical for a moment. If you're ready to dive in, here are some actionable steps to kickstart your philanthropic journey. First, assess your resources—time, money, and skills. Determine what you're willing to contribute. Next, identify causes that resonate with you. Research organizations doing impactful work in those areas. Reach out, get involved, and learn more about their initiatives.

Consider setting specific goals for your giving. Whether it's a dollar amount or a number of volunteer hours, having clear objectives will help you stay focused and motivated. Monitor your progress and adjust as needed. Celebrate the successes, both big and small.

Explore various giving vehicles. You could consider donor-advised funds, which allow you to make a charitable contribution, receive an immediate tax deduction, and then recommend grants to your chosen charities over time. This provides flexibility while maximizing your impact.

Stay informed about the social and environmental issues that matter to you. Read articles, attend conferences, and engage in discussions. The more knowledgeable you are, the more effective you'll be as a philanthropist.

And remember, it's not just about the money. If you have skills or expertise, consider offering pro bono work to organizations that align with your values. Whether it's providing legal advice, marketing support, or mentorship, your time can be just as valuable as financial contributions.

As you navigate this journey, never lose sight of your "why." Why are you giving? What drives your passion? Keeping your purpose at the forefront will not only fuel your philanthropic efforts but also inspire others to join you.

Let's switch gears and talk about the concept of "triple bottom line." This idea emphasizes that businesses should focus not only on profit but also on people and the planet. As you accumulate wealth, consider how your business practices align with these principles. Are you making ethical decisions? Are you contributing to a sustainable future?

This shift in mindset can lead to a more holistic approach to wealth-building. It's about recognizing that your financial success is interconnected with social and environmental well-being. When you make decisions that prioritize people and the planet, you're not just protecting your wealth; you're contributing to a thriving world.

Now, let's touch on the idea of global impact. In our interconnected world, challenges often cross borders. Consider supporting international causes that resonate with you. This might involve funding education initiatives in developing countries, supporting healthcare access in underserved regions, or contributing to environmental conservation efforts worldwide.

The impact of your contributions can be magnified when you think globally. Collaborate with international organizations that align with your values. Engage in initiatives that promote social justice, environmental sustainability, and economic development across the globe. Your wealth can be a force for good beyond your immediate community.

As we wrap up this discussion, remember that philanthropy and social impact are not just for the wealthy elite. They're for everyone who wants to make a difference. Whether you start small or dive in headfirst, your contributions matter.

Wealth is a tool, and how you choose to wield it defines your legacy. Embrace the opportunity to create positive change in the world. Engage with your community, support causes that resonate with you, and inspire others to join the movement.

Your journey into philanthropy doesn't have to be perfect. It's about progress, learning, and growing along the way. You'll face challenges, but those hurdles can lead to breakthroughs and innovations. As you embark on this path, stay true to your values, keep your purpose in mind, and let your actions speak louder than words.

In the end, it's about understanding that true wealth is measured not just in dollars and cents but in the impact you make on the lives of others. As you navigate your financial journey, let philanthropy be your compass—a guiding force that drives you to create a better, more equitable world. When you get rich enough to question the meaning of money, remember: it's about what you do with it that truly counts.

6.1 Cultivating Meaningful Relationships

Let's dive into the heartbeat of success—relationships. No amount of money can substitute for the power of meaningful connections. Wealth isn't just about the cash flow; it's about the people who stand beside you, the mentors who guide you, and the networks you build. When you get rich enough to question the meaning of money, you'll realize that the real treasure lies in your relationships.

First off, think about the people in your life. Who are you surrounding yourself with? Are they lifting you up, challenging you, pushing you to grow? If not, it's time for a reevaluation. You need a circle that inspires you, not just friends who nod along with everything you say.

Relationships are like investments. You want to put your time and energy into those that yield the highest returns. Seek out individuals who align with your values, share your vision, and bring something unique to the table. These are the people who will challenge you when you need it and celebrate your wins with you. They become your tribe.

Let's talk about networking. Most people think of networking as handing out business cards at events and making small talk. That's the bare minimum. Real networking is about building authentic connections. It's about engaging in conversations that matter, understanding people's stories, and finding ways to support one another. When you approach networking as a relationship-building exercise, it transforms the experience.

The best way to cultivate these relationships is to start with genuine curiosity. Ask questions, listen actively, and show that you care. This doesn't mean you have to dive deep into someone's life story on the first meeting, but show interest. What motivates them? What challenges are they facing? The more you learn about others, the more you can find common ground.

Then there's vulnerability. Don't be afraid to share your own journey—the highs, the lows, the lessons learned. Vulnerability builds trust. When you open up, it invites others to do the same. It's in these moments of authenticity that real connections are formed. People remember how you made them feel, not just what you said.

A powerful tool in relationship-building is gratitude. A simple "thank you" can go a long way. Acknowledge the people who've helped you along the way. Whether it's a mentor, a friend, or even a stranger who offered a piece of advice, let them know their impact. Gratitude creates positive energy and strengthens bonds. It's contagious—spread it like wildfire.

Now, let's get tactical. Schedule regular check-ins with your connections. This doesn't have to be formal—a quick coffee, a phone call, or even a text to see how they're doing. Consistency matters. People appreciate being remembered, and those little gestures reinforce your commitment to the relationship.

You should also be proactive about offering value. Think about what you can give rather than what you can get. Can you introduce someone to a potential client? Share an article that might interest them? Offer advice based on your own experiences? The more you give, the more you'll receive in return. This isn't about transactional relationships; it's about cultivating a culture of support and generosity.

When it comes to building a network, diversify. Don't just connect with people in your industry. Seek out those from different backgrounds, experiences, and professions. This diversity enriches your perspective and opens up new opportunities. You never know where a conversation with someone outside your field might lead.

Don't underestimate the power of online relationships, especially in today's digital age. Platforms like LinkedIn, Twitter, and even Instagram can help you connect with like-minded individuals. Engage with their content, join discussions, and share your insights. Building an online presence allows you to extend your reach beyond your immediate circle. Just remember, the key is authenticity. Don't just scroll; engage.

As you build relationships, be mindful of your brand. Your reputation precedes you, so ensure that you're living up to the values you want to represent. Be known for your integrity, your willingness to help, and your commitment to growth. Your brand is what people will talk about when you're not in the room.

Now, let's not forget about mentorship. Finding a mentor can be a game-changer. Look for someone who's been where you want to go. This person can offer insights, guidance, and support. But remember, mentorship is a two-way street. Don't just take; be willing to give back. Even if you feel you don't have much to offer yet, your enthusiasm and willingness to learn can be incredibly valuable.

On the flip side, consider being a mentor yourself. Sharing your knowledge and experiences can be incredibly rewarding. You get to help others while reinforcing your own understanding. Mentoring is a way to give back, and it strengthens your own network. Plus, there's something fulfilling about seeing someone grow because of your guidance.

Now, let's talk about the importance of community. Being part of a community creates a sense of belonging. Find groups, organizations, or clubs that align with your interests and values. This not only expands your network but also connects you with people who share your passions. It's an opportunity to learn, grow, and collaborate.

In any relationship, communication is key. Be clear about your intentions and expectations. Misunderstandings can create unnecessary tension. Approach conversations with openness and honesty. If you're facing challenges, don't shy away from addressing them. Open dialogue can strengthen bonds and build trust.

When it comes to building relationships, be intentional. This means being strategic about how you invest your time and energy. Identify the key players in your life—those who inspire you, challenge you, and support your growth. Prioritize these relationships and invest in them consistently.

Be patient. Relationships take time to develop. Don't expect instant results. Nurturing connections is like tending to a garden. You have to water it, give it sunlight, and allow it to grow. Some relationships may flourish quickly, while others may take longer. Trust the process.

Don't forget to celebrate milestones together. Whether it's a personal achievement or a business success, share the joy. A simple congratulatory message can strengthen your bond. When you take the time to celebrate others, it shows that you care about their success as much as your own.

Another essential aspect of meaningful relationships is accountability. Surround yourself with people who will hold you accountable for your goals. Share your aspirations, and ask them to check in on your progress. This not only keeps you focused but also fosters a supportive environment where everyone is striving for growth.

When it comes to expanding your network, don't shy away from reaching out to those you admire. If there's someone you want to connect with, send them a message. Express your appreciation for their work, share your thoughts, and see if they're open to a conversation. You'd be surprised how many people are willing to connect, especially if you approach it with authenticity and respect.

Networking events can be daunting, but they're also opportunities to forge meaningful connections. When you attend these events, have a plan. Set specific goals—maybe it's to meet three new people or to have a deep conversation with someone you admire. Approach the event with intention, and follow up with those you connect with.

As you navigate relationships, don't forget the importance of follow-through. If you say you're going to do something—whether it's sending an article, making an introduction, or checking in—make sure you follow through. Consistency builds trust, and it reinforces your commitment to the relationship.

The role of empathy cannot be overstated. As you build relationships, practice empathy. Put yourself in others' shoes. Understand their perspectives, challenges, and motivations. When you approach relationships with empathy, you create deeper connections. People feel valued and understood, which fosters a sense of belonging.

In today's fast-paced world, people often rush through interactions. Slow down. Take the time to truly connect. Engage in meaningful conversations. Ask thought-provoking questions, and listen actively. Quality over quantity is key. It's better to have a few deep relationships than a long list of superficial connections.

When you get into the groove of cultivating relationships, you'll notice something: it's infectious. When you treat people well, they often pay it forward. You create a ripple effect of positivity that extends beyond your immediate circle. This is how you build a community that thrives on support, collaboration, and growth.

As you become more successful, you might encounter jealousy or resentment from others. It's a reality that comes with growth. Don't let that deter you. Stay focused on your journey, and remember that your success doesn't diminish others' worth. Be gracious, celebrate others, and lift those around you.

The power of storytelling is immense in relationship-building. When you share your story—your struggles, triumphs, and lessons learned—you create a connection. People resonate with authenticity. Your experiences can inspire others and open the door for meaningful conversations.

In a world dominated by social media, be mindful of how you use it. Social platforms can be a double-edged sword. They can help you connect but can also create a facade of connection. Use social media to engage genuinely, share your insights, and celebrate others' successes. Avoid falling into the trap of comparison.

Let's talk about gratitude again—this time, in a more proactive way. Consider creating a gratitude practice. Regularly reflect on the people who've made a difference in your life. Write them a note, send them a message, or simply express your appreciation when you see them. A little gratitude goes a long way in strengthening bonds.

Lastly, be open to change. As you grow, so will your relationships. Some connections may fade, while new ones will blossom. Embrace the evolution of your network. Life is a journey, and the people you meet along the way shape your path.

As you cultivate meaningful relationships, remember that this is a lifelong journey. It requires effort, intention, and a genuine desire to connect. When you focus on building authentic connections, you not only enrich your life but also create a network of support that propels you toward your goals.

When you get rich enough to question the meaning of money, you'll find that it's the relationships you've built that provide the most profound sense of fulfillment. Money is a tool; relationships are what create a life worth living. So go out there, connect with people, nurture those relationships, and watch how they elevate your life beyond wealth.

6.2 Redefining Success and Legacy

To put it bluntly, most individuals have a distorted idea of what success really entails. Words like "money," "status," and "fame" are used by society as if they are the ultimate goal. The reality is that success is much more than having a large financial account. It all comes down to your legacy and the influence you leave. When you begin to wonder what money really means, you come to see that true riches isn't only material; rather, it's about the lives you've impacted, the people you've affected, and the world you've helped.

Consider it. How would you define success? You're missing the wider picture if your only goal is to increase your income. Indeed, having financial independence is wonderful—who doesn't want to wake up without having to worry about their bills? True success, however, is more complex. It's about purpose, fulfillment, and the connections you make along the path. You may change your focus from acquisition to contributing by redefining success.

Let's talk about legacy honestly. When you're gone, what do you want others to say about you? That you were wealthy? Or that you had an impact? Your legacy is the impression you make on the world. It's the tales people share about you, the things you taught them, and the motivation you gave them. You must start looking beyond yourself if you want to leave a lasting impact.

Considering your values is a potent method to redefine success. What do you believe in? Which values serve as your compass? You risk having a ton of money but a hollow spirit if you pursue achievement without having a clear understanding of your beliefs. Everything changes when your actions reflect your ideals. All of a sudden, success is determined not just by your financial situation but also by how well you're living in line with your own values.

Let's now discuss the significance of purpose. You risk burning out if all you're doing is working for money. However, everything changes when you have a driving purpose. You're on a mission, so you wake up eager to take on the day. Real success comes from pursuing your passion, which is fueled by your mission. When you link your job to your mission, whether it be to assist others, create something beautiful, or challenge the status quo, you're headed toward a satisfying existence.

Let us now confront the unspoken issue of social pressure. The pressure to pursue traditional achievement is quite strong. You "live the dream" after graduating, finding employment, and purchasing a home. What if, however, that dream doesn't speak to you? What if your course appears to be different? Accept that. Your path is entirely your own. Redefining success entails defying social expectations and establishing your own criteria.

It's simple to slip into the comparison trap in the social media age. You feel like you're not accomplishing enough when you see other people showing off their accomplishments. Just stop there. Keep in mind that what you read online is frequently a summary rather than the whole picture. Pay attention to your development and adventure. Success is a personal journey rather than a sprint.

Let's discuss satisfaction. What makes you happy? Which tasks cause you to lose track of time? You will experience fulfillment when your employment is in line with your passions. It's time to change course if your everyday routine seems tedious. Success is about flourishing, not about suffering. Make room in your life for the things that bring you joy.

Mentoring is one of the most effective methods to leave a lasting legacy. Consider the individuals you have impacted, either directly or indirectly. In addition to influencing others' futures, mentoring upholds your principles and goals. It's a means to give back, impart your wisdom, and assist others in avoiding the mistakes you made. Your influence can go much beyond the people in your immediate vicinity.

Let's now examine how appreciation might be used to redefine success. Your perspective changes as you concentrate on your blessings. You begin to value the experience, the people in your life, and the knowledge you've gained. Being grateful helps you stay grounded and remember that success isn't just determined by your accomplishments but also by the circumstances that have shaped you. Honor little triumphs. Recognize other people's contributions. This cultivates a culture of gratitude that may be included into your legacy.

Think on the concept of plenty as you reconsider success. All too frequently, individuals think in terms of scarcity. They hoard success because they think there can only be so much of it. Contrarily, abundance is the understanding that there is enough for everyone. You're more likely to impart your knowledge, encourage others, and have a beneficial impact on the world when you live with an abundant attitude. This not only increases your own achievement but also multiplies your legacy through a cascading impact.

Let's talk about the value of community while we're on the subject of ripple effects. Your legacy is influenced by the connections you make. Be in the company of individuals who push you, encourage you, and help you develop. You improve yourself when you uplift others. A robust community serves as a potent basis for achievement and legacy. Cooperate, exchange ideas, and strive toward shared objectives. This group energy increases your influence and broadens your audience.

Let's talk about effect now. What type of world change are you hoping to bring about? You change the story when you consider success in terms of effect. Contributing to something greater is more important than focusing only on one's own interests. Think about how you can make a lasting difference in someone's life, whether it be via community service, philanthropy, or just being a positive influence.

Remember resilience as well. Success doesn't always come easily. You will encounter difficulties, disappointments, and roadblocks. Your journey is defined by how you handle these obstacles. Long-term success depends on developing resilience. Consider each setback you have as a teaching moment. What makes you unique is your capacity to recover and keep going.

Let us shift our focus to the concept of lifelong learning. Success is a journey rather than a destination. Be open to new experiences, maintain your curiosity, and pursue knowledge. When you hit a specific financial milestone, your progress doesn't stop. Keep pushing yourself, developing your abilities, and changing. In addition to enhancing your life, a dedication to continual learning serves as a potent role model for others.

As you strive for achievement, you should also consider your legacy. Which values do you wish to inculcate in other people? Think about the tales you would like others to tell about you. Character is more important than accomplishments alone. In what way would you like to be remembered? You may use this reflection to help you make decisions that will help you leave the legacy you want.

Let's discuss creativity. Success is frequently associated with traditional paths, such as business, finance, etc. However, innovation might change your perspective of success. Give yourself permission to think creatively. Take chances, experiment, and be creative. As much as traditional commercial initiatives, artistic endeavors may lead to success. A key component of making your imprint is embracing your imagination.

Redefining success may also be greatly aided by networking. Create relationships not just for your own benefit but also to share your expertise and learn from others. Working together with others who think differently broadens your horizons and helps you develop in ways you never would have imagined. Every relationship has the capacity to provide new perspectives that might change the way you perceive success.

Lastly, keep in mind that the process of determining legacy and success is a continuous one. It's an ongoing process rather than a one-time choice. Your objectives may change, your interests may change, and your values may change. Accept this flexibility. Every stage of life offers fresh insights and chances for development.

Think on values, purpose, fulfillment, community, influence, resilience, and lifelong learning as you reflect on your path. These are the cornerstones of a reimagined definition of success. You'll find that success is more about who you become and the legacy you leave behind than it is about what you do when you include these aspects into your life.

Let these ideas serve as a guide for you when you start to wonder what money really means. Success is more than just a figure in your bank account; it's the legacy you leave behind, the lives you change, and the influence you make. Your quest is about significance, not simply money. And that's where life's real richness is found.

Conclusion

Let's take a moment to be honest. You have just embarked on a quest to redefine success, riches, and what it means to be happy. You have gained knowledge on changing one's perspective, adding value, increasing revenue, being financially literate, and developing meaningful relationships. The worst part is that this isn't a one-time read. It's time to bring everything together; it's a continuous journey.

Money is a tool. That's all. It doesn't quantify your value or describe who you are. I've been emphasizing this issue because it's really important. You begin to understand that genuine wealth is about experiences, connections, and effect when you reach a point of financial success where you may start to wonder what money really means. It's about what you leave behind and how you present yourself to the world.

Consider it. What will you recall when you reflect on your life? Does it have to do with the cash signs, or with the time you spent with loved ones, the obstacles you surmounted, and the people you assisted? Life is a compilation of tales, lessons, and memories rather than a financial statement. And they are the important things.

Let's now discuss value generation. This is where it all begins. Consider how you may help others if you want to create lasting riches. Seek out market gaps, comprehend problems, and come up with creative fixes. You'll have more chances to make money the more value you produce. This has to do with life, not just business. In your profession, relationships, or community, approach every connection with the intention of adding value.

It is likewise impossible to overlook the significance of resilience. You will undoubtedly encounter challenges. What distinguishes you is how you react. Every failure is a chance to improve, and every setback is a lesson. Accept the difficulties. They are stepping stones rather than obstacles. The most successful individuals I know have been the ones who have failed miserably but have gotten back up, picked themselves up, and continued on.

The idea of legacy comes next. What you leave behind is just as important as what you accomplish. When considering your legacy, consider what you would like to be known for. Making money is insufficient; you also need to think about how your activities affect other people. Are you improving the state of the world? Do you encourage those around you? The richness of life goes well beyond material achievement if you concentrate on leaving a lasting legacy.

Now let's discuss the relationships. They serve as the foundation for everything. You are not a haven. Your success, your attitude, and your energy are influenced by the people you spend time with. Take care of those connections. Take the time to cultivate your network. Create a community that encourages you and pushes you to improve. These relationships, whether they be friends, coworkers, or mentors, enhance your life and provide opportunities you were unaware of.

We must now remember personal development. This trip lasts a lifetime. Keep your curiosity alive. Continue to learn. Look for novel experiences. Push yourself. Growth occurs when you venture into the unknown rather than in your comfort zone. Your success is enhanced by each new ability you get and each lesson you learn. You want to continue developing and improving as a person.

Given how important financial literacy is, let's discuss it once more. Making money isn't enough; you also need to know how to handle it. Know how to save wealth, budget, and invest. Your knowledge of finance is a strength in and of itself. You get greater power the more you understand. Additionally, that empowerment enables you to make more informed choices that are consistent with your objectives and beliefs.

Additionally, you should prioritize social impact and philanthropy. When you're wealthy enough to be able to give back, do it. Help individuals in need, support causes you care about, and have an influence on your community. This is about leaving a legacy of giving and kindness, not simply about charity. Often, the satisfaction of giving back outweighs any potential financial advantage.

Remember to reinterpret what success means to you as you travel this path. Don't allow society tell you what to do. Your idea of success should align with your mission, beliefs, and interests. Success comes naturally when your activities are in line with your own priorities.

Think about your goal. What motivates you? What thrills you? Everything changes when your employment is in line with your mission. You'll be passionate and prepared to take on any challenge when you get up each day. Nowadays, success is a delight rather than a chore.

Being aware of your mental state is crucial in this endeavor. Your experiences will be changed by adopting a growth-oriented, optimistic mentality. Consider obstacles as chances for personal development rather than as insurmountable obstacles. This change in perspective enables you to overcome challenges. head-on and keeps you on course to achieve your objectives.

Lastly, never undervalue the importance of thankfulness. It may sound cliche, but cultivating thankfulness transforms everything. Recognizing your blessings causes you to change your perspective from what you lack to what you have in abundance. This kind of thinking not only makes you happier, but it also draws in new possibilities. The more you value what you already have, the more you make room for more.

What's the lesson here, then? It all comes down to perception. You begin to view the world differently when you start to wonder what money really means. You come to see that concentrating on adding value, fostering connections, and having an influence makes life richer. The lives you impact and the legacy you leave behind are just as valuable as the money you earn.

Put all of this information to use. Make minor adjustments first. Change your perspective, put value first, make connections, and make a commitment to lifelong learning. You'll be surprised by the outcome. You'll discover that leading a fulfilling, impactful, and purposeful life is where real riches is found.

Remember that it's more important to focus on who you become along the road than where you end up as you continue your journey beyond prosperity. Accept the difficulties, rejoice at the successes, and never lose sight of the important things. You have the entire world at your disposal. Go out there and design a life that represents the depth of your connections, experiences, and legacy while simultaneously challenging the notion that money is meaningful.

www.ingramcontent.com/pod-product-compliance
Lightning Source LLC
LaVergne TN
LVHW022310200926
848481LV00004B/1270
* 9 7 9 8 2 3 1 4 2 5 7 4 7 *